100 Great Monologues

from the

Neo-Classical Theater

Smith and Kraus *Books For Actors*
THE MONOLOGUE SERIES
The Best Men's/Women's Stage Monologues of 1993
The Best Men's/Women's Stage Monologues of 1992
The Best Men's/Women's Stage Monologues of 1991
The Best Men's/Women's Stage Monologues of 1990
One Hundred Men's/Women's Stage Monologues from the 1980's
2 Minutes and Under: Character Monologues for Actors
Street Talk: Character Monologues for Actors
Uptown: Character Monologues for Actors
Monologues from Contemporary Literature: Volume I
Monologues from Classic Plays 468 B.C. to 1960 A.D.
FESTIVAL MONOLOGUE SERIES
The Great Monologues from the Humana Festival
The Great Monologues from the EST Marathon
The Great Monologues from the Women's Project
The Great Monologues from the Mark Taper Forum
YOUNG ACTORS SERIES
Great Scenes and Monologues for Children
New Plays from A.C.T.'s Young Conservatory
Great Scenes for Young Actors from the Stage
Great Monologues for Young Actors
Multicultural Monologues for Young Actors
Multicultural Scenes for Young Actors
SCENE STUDY SERIES
Scenes From Classic Plays 468 B.C. to 1970 A.D.
The Best Stage Scenes of 1993
The Best Stage Scenes of 1992
The Best Stage Scenes for Men/Women from the 1980's
CONTEMPORARY PLAYWRIGHTS
Romulus Linney: 17 Short Plays
Eric Overmyer: Collected Plays
Lanford Wilson: 21 Short Plays
William Mastrosimone: Collected Plays
Horton Foote: 4 New Plays
Israel Horovitz: 16 Short Plays
Terrence McNally: 15 Short Plays
Women Playwrights: The Best Plays of 1993
Women Playwrights: The Best Plays of 1992
Humana Festival '94: The Complete Plays
Humana Festival '93: The Complete Plays
GREAT TRANSLATION FOR ACTORS SERIES
The Wood Demon: Anton Chekhov *translated by N. Saunders & F. Dwyer*
The Sea Gull *translated by N. Saunders & F. Dwyer*
Three Sisters: Anton Chekhov *translated by Lanford Wilson*
OTHER BOOKS IN OUR COLLECTION
The Actor's Chekhov
Kiss and Tell: Restoration Scenes, Monologues, & History
Cold Readings: Some Do's and Don'ts for Actors at Auditions

If you require pre-publication information about upcoming Smith and Kraus books, you may receive our semi-annual catalogue, free of charge, by sending your name and address to *Smith and Kraus Catalogue, One Main Street, PO Box 127, Lyme, NH 03768.*
Telephone 800.895.4331 Fax 603.795.4427.

100 GREAT MONOLOGUES

from the
Neo-Classical Theater

edited by Jocelyn A. Beard

Monologue Audition Series

SK
A Smith and Kraus Book

Published by Smith and Kraus, Inc.
One Main Street, Lyme, NH 03768

Copyright © 1994 by Smith and Kraus, Inc.
All rights reserved
Manufactured in the United States of America

First Edition: November 1994
10 9 8 7 6 5 4 3 2

NOTE: These monologues are intended to be used for audition and class study; permission is not required to use the material for those purposes.

Library of Congress Cataloging-in-Publication Data

100 great monologues from the neo-classical theatre / edited by Jocelyn A. Beard.
--1st ed.
        p.   cm. -- (Monologue audition series)
    ISBN 1-880399-60-1 : $8.95

1. Monologues. 2. Acting--Auditions. 3. European drama--17th century--Translations into English. 4. English drama--18th century. I Beard, Jocelyn.
II. Title: One hundred great monologues from the neo-classical theatre.
III. Series.

PN2080.A126   1994
808.82'45--dc20   94-33114
                                                    CIP

I would like to dedicate this book
to Mary Jane Phelan, Beth Bonnabeau-Harding,
Francis Arnold Daley, Joe Harding and John Critides
with untold thanks
for their amazing efforts on my behalf.
Thanks guys!

—Jocelyn A. Beard

Contents

MEN'S MONOLOGUES

Foreword

Boy, was this book a bear to put together! I know what you're thinking: Poor Jocelyn gets paid to sit at home and read plays...boo hoo! Boo hoo, indeed. Reading through the theatre of the Restoration and Neo-Classical eras was absolutely exhausting. No, scratch "exhausting" and change it to "mind-numbing." You try reading nothing but Moliere, Vanbrugh, Racine and Dryden for a couple of months and see what happens to your brain! Sure, the stuff is great—some say the greatest—but it's fast, and I do mean fast. No lingering monologues full of deep sentiment and pertinent historical data here! The characters of the British Restoration and French Enlightenment lived in a world that was changing faster than the playwrights—some of the keenest wits in history—could keep up with. These are characters of the senses who seem so much more accessible than the intellectual manifestations of the Renaissance theatre. Bawdy and lewd, the theatre of the restoration provoked both amusement and outrage in a society poised on the brink of accepting it as an institution.

The Restoration arrived right on the heels of the late Renaissance, and with it some of the most sparkling and acerbic wits to ever lend their voices to the stage. Writers like Dryden, Congreve and Wycherley created biting new pieces of theatre that spared no expense in their efforts to satirize society and its licentious nature. Comedy and drama alike targeted the ever-evolving relationship between men and women by placing characters in outrageously compromised positions, much to the delight of the audiences of the day.

And then it happened: The Age of Reason. Can you for a single moment imagine that any human being at any time in history looked around him or herself and said: "Yup, this is it: The Age of Reason."? Well, thank goodness we had one, because as a precursor to the Age of Revolution, the Age of Reason served to reawaken a thirst for classical themes and styles. Plays like *Andromache*, *Phedre* and *All For Love* served to remind us of the glorious days of antiquity when the subject—the only subject—of art was man. Neo-Classicism was born, and with it, the debate between the Ancients and the Moderns. The Ancients craved the order and beauty of the classical world whereas the Moderns lusted for a new world that only change would bring. anyone hanging around Philadelphia or Paris in 1776 and 1789 respectively could tell you which of the two factions got their wish.

And so I leave you, in these most pivotal of years, to immerse yourself in the lightning-paced theatre of the restoration and the clearly-drawn theatre of the Neo-Classical writers. If you liken would theatre to the pounding surf, then the theatre of the Renaissance is a wave as it crashes mightily on the beach in an explosion of long pent-up words and ideas. The Theatre of the restoration is the wave as it quickly recedes away from the shore, pulling more and more writers along with it, and the Theatre of Neo-Classicism is the wave as it draws up silently; a thing of power and beauty, waiting to crash yet again…but that the third volume: 19th Century Romantic and Realistic Theatres.

Break A Leg!

Jocelyn A. Beard
Summer 1994
Patterson, New York

100 GREAT MONOLOGUES

from the

Neo-Classical Theatre

Women's Monologues

All for Love or
The World Well Lost

John Dryden
1678

Scene: Alexandria

Dramatic

Cleopatra: Queen of Egypt, 30–40

Mark Antony has moved out of their palace quarters and taken up solitary residence in the Temple of Isis. His old friend and fellow Roman, Ventidius, has convinced him to leave Cleopatra and fight Octavius. Here, the Queen mourns her lover's departure.

CLEOPATRA: I am no queen:
Is this to be a queen, to be so besieged
By yon insulting Roman, and to wait
Each hour the victor's chain? These ills are small:
For Antony is lost, and I can mourn
For nothing else but him. Now come, Octavius,
I have no more to lose; prepare thy bands;
I'm fit to be a captive: Antony
Has taught my mind the fortune of a slave.
[*IRAS:* Call reason to assist you.]
CLEOPATRA: I have none,
And none would have: my love's a noble madness,
Which shows the cause deserved it. Moderate sorrow
Fits vulgar love, and for a vulgar man:
But I have loved with such transcendent passion,
I soared, at first, quite out of reason's view,
And now am lost above it. No, I'm proud
'Tis thus; would Antony could see me now!
Think you he would not sigh? Though he must leave me,
Sure he would sigh; for he is noble-natured,
And bears a tender heart: I know him well.
Ah, no, I know him not; I knew him once,
But now 'tis past.
[*IRAS:* Let it be past with you: Forget him, madam.]

1

CLEOPATRA: Never, never, Iras.
He once was mine; and once, though now 'tis gone,
Leaves a faint image of possession still.
.[*ALEX:* Think him unconstant, cruel, and ungrateful.]
CLEOPATRA: I cannot: if I could, those thoughts were vain,
Faithless, ungrateful, cruel, though he be,
I still must love him.

Andromache

Jean Racine
1667

Scene: Epirus, after the fall of Troy

Dramatic

Hermione: the daughter of Helen of Troy, 20s

Hermione has betrayed Pyrrhus, the man she loves, who has forsaken her to marry the captive Andromache. The vengeful Hermione has persuaded Orestes, the Greek Ambassador, to murder Pyrrhus. Here, she anticipates the news of his death.

HERMIONE: Where am I? What is this that I have done?
And now,—do what? What frenzies clutch at me?
I wander through these halls, I know not whither.
I am destroyed with grief! I do not know
If I do love or hate him! When he left me,
His eyes,—they seemed to freeze my very soul.
He would not even look as if he pitied.
No, not a moment's tenderness or sorrow!
His heart would never grant one cry to me.
He could not hear my sighing. He was calm
Through all my agony, and all my tears
Could wake no sympathy. And yet I mourn!
To crown its sorrow, this poor heart still throbs
Only for him. The blow will soon be struck.
I tremble at it; I forget revenge.
Indeed I think I almost might forgive him!
No, I shall not call my sentence back.
The traitor dies, since he is dead to me!
He laughs in triumph, and he scorns my anger,
Thinks it a storm that will be spent in tears,
That I am always weak, that I will waver,
That my own hand will shield him from my blows!
I have been kind; he thinks it has no bounds!
And there are other thoughts to fill his mind.
The traitor, in his triumph, does not care
Whether the absent wish him life or death,

And leaves this great perplexity to me!
But one stroke ends it! By Orestes' hand
He meets the death that he might well have looked for,
Which I desire, because he made me wish it!
Then is it I who must pronounce his doom?
He dies because Hermione has loved him?—
He whose great deeds were told and told again,
To give me new delight whene'er I heard them?—
To whom I'd bound my fate, all secretly,
Before they tied us, by that fatal bond?
And have I crossed so many lands and seas,
Coming so far only to dig his grave,
To be his murdered? Before he dies—

The Beaux Stratagem

George Farquhar
1707

Scene: Lichfield

Dramatic
>   Mrs. Sullen: an unhappy wife, 20–30

>   Squire Sullen is a terrible husband whose coarse and brutish ways have driven his
>   wife to despair. Here, she confesses to his sister her desire to end her marriage.

MRS. SULLEN: Patience! the cant of custom—Providence sends no evil
without a remedy. Should I lie groaning under a yoke I can shake off, I
were accessory to my ruin, and my patience were no better than self-
murder.

[*DORINDA:* But how can you shake off the yoke? Your divisions don't
come within the reach of the law for a divorce.]

MRS. SULLEN: Law! what law can search into the remote abyss of nature? What evidence can prove the unaccountable disaffections of wedlock? Can a jury sum up the endless aversions that are rooted in our
souls, or can a bench give judgment upon antipathies?

[*DORINDA:* They never pretended, sister; they never meddle, but in
case of uncleanness.]

MRS. SULLEN: Uncleanness! O sister! casual violation is a transient injury, and may possibly be repaired; but can radical hatreds be ever rec-
onciled? No, no, sister; Nature is the first lawgiver; and when she has
set tempers opposite, not all the golden links of wedlock nor iron manacles of law can keep 'em fast.[1]

Wedlock we own ordained by Heaven's decree,

---

1. Mrs. Sullen's speeches with Milton's *Doctrine and Discipline of Divorce*: "God sends reme-
dies, as well as evils; under which he who lies and groans, that may lawfully acquit himself,
is accessory to his own ruin: nor will it excuse him though he suffer, through a sluggish
fearfulness to search thoroughly what is lawful, for fear of disquieting the secure falsity of
an old opinion" (p. 341). God did not authorize "a judicial court to toss about and divulge
the unaccountable and secret reasons of disaffection between man and wife" (p. 343). "Casual adultery . . . [is] but a transient injury, and soon amended," but "natural hatred" is "an
unspeakable and unremitting sorrow and offence, whereof no amends can be made, no
cure, no ceasing but by divorce" (pp 332–33). "To couple hatred therefore, though wedlock
try all her golden links, and borrow to her aid all the iron manacles and fetters of law, it
does but seek to twist a rope of sand" (p. 345).

But such as Heaven ordained it first to be—
Concurring tempers in the man and wife
As mutual helps to draw the load of life.
View all the works of Providence above:
The stars with harmony and concord move;
View all the works of Providence below:
The fire, the water, earth and air, we know,
All in one plant agree to make it grow.
Must man, the chiefest work of art divine,
Be doomed in endless discord to repine?
No, we should injure Heaven by that surmise:
Omnipotence is just, were man but wise.

The Burial of Danish Comedy

Ludvig Holberg

1727

Scene: a theater

Serio-Comic
>Thalia: the muse, any age

> Lack of funds forced Holberg to close the Lille Grønnegade Theatre in 1727. This play was written to commemorate that sad event. This speech, performed by Thalia, the muse of the theatre, is a bittersweet and eternally pertinent statement.

THALIA: With head held high, I swept onstage, in colorful
>resplendence.

Now mourning clothes and lowered head replace that once-grand
>entrance.

Once a birthday celebration, now a funeral cortege;

Once heaven showered blessings, now it's havoc and distress.

Heaven smiled the first year—our Golden Days, perhaps.

We almost feared that we would see the gallery collapse.

The squeeze began the second year, as funds began to dwindle.

The third year was in credit's grasp, bills mounting on the spindle.

Some left for Jutland, Funen, Norway as hunger drove us blind,

And Toyon[2] threatened to withhold every single drop of wine.

The tradesmen soon began to frown with each successive debit

On our account. They finally said, "Nothing more on credit!"

We wrote promissory notes, but no one would accept them.

All returned them with an oath to utterly reject them.

We offered to post liens against the year's projected income.

To no avail—though we cajoled and begged and pled and then some.

Even Sons of Israel, who for three times normal usury

Are moved to some compassion, rejected our last surety.

It didn't matter if the bills were notarized or plain,

It was enough for Henrich and Pernille[3] to be named.

[2]Mathieu Toyon was a Gascon Frenchman who owned a pub and wine business near the theatre on Pilestræde.

[3]Names of the beloved servants in most Holberg comedies, here used to indicate all bills for the Lille Grønnegade Theatre, whether written on official "stamped" or ordinary paper.

And so we've lived and suffered: hunger, debt, exposure;
Teetering between debtor's prison and foreclosure,
Till the Comedy fell victim to its final deadly curse,
From intermittent fever, gone the way of all the earth.

Cato

Joseph Addison
1713

Scene: Utica

Dramatic

> Lucia: Daughter of Lucius, a Roman statesman in exile, 18–20

> Lucia's father was the best friend of Cato, the fallen hero of Rome. She was in love with Cato's son, Marcus who was killed in battle. Here, the grieving Lucia offers insight into the frustrating role that women must play in a world swept along by male politics.

LUCIA: What odd fantastic things we women do!
Who would not listen when young lovers woo?
But die a maid, yet have the choice of two!
Ladies are often cruel to their cost;
To give you pain, themselves they punish most.
Vows of virginity should well be weigh'd;
Too oft they're cancell'd, though in convents made.
Would you revenge such rash resolves—you may:
Be spiteful—and believe the thing we say;
We hate you when you're easily said nay.
How needless, if you knew us, were your fears!
Let love have eyes, and beauty will have ears.
Our hearts are form'd, as you yourselves would choose,
Too proud to ask, too humble to refuse:
We give to merit, and to wealth we sell;
He sighs with most success that settles well.
The woes of wedlock with the joys we mix;
'Tis best repenting in a coach and six.
      Blame not our conduct, since we but pursue
Those lively lessons we have learn'd from you:
Your breasts no more the fire of beauty warms,
But wicked wealth usurps the power of charms;
What pains to get the gaudy thing you hate,
To swell in show, and be a wretch in state!
At plays you ogle, at the Ring you bow;
Ev'n churches are no sanctuaries now.

There, golden idols all your vows receive;
She is no goddess that has nought to give.
Oh, may once more the happy age appear,
When words were artless, and the thoughts sincere;
When gold and grandeur were unenvy'd things,
And courts less coveted than groves and springs.
Love then shall only mourn when truth complains,
And constancy feel transport in its chains.
Sighs with success their own soft anguish tell,
And eyes shall utter what the lips conceal:
Virtue again to its bright station climb,
And beauty fear no enemy but time.
The fair shall listen to desert alone,
And every Lucia find a Cato's son.

The Careless Husband

Colley Cibber
1705

Scene: Windsor

Dramatic
> Lady Easy: A long-suffering wife, 20–30

> When Lady Easy discovers her husband with her maid, she forces herself to remember her vow of obedience.

LADY EASY: Ha!
Protect me virtue, patience, reason!
Teach me to bear this killing sight, or let
Me think my dreaming senses are deceived!
For sure a sight like this might raise the arm
Of duty, even to the breast of love. At least
I'll throw this vizor of my patience off,
Now wake him in his guilt,
And barefaced front him with my wrongs.
I'll talk to him till he blushes, nay till he
Frowns on me, perhaps—and then
I'm lost again. The ease of a few tears
Is all that's left to me—
And duty, too, forbids me to insult
Where I have vowed obedience. Perhaps
The fault's in me, and nature has not formed
Me with the thousand little requisites
That warm the heart to love.
Somewhere there is a fault,
But heaven best knows what both of us deserve.
Ha! Bareheaded and in so sound a sleep!
Who knows, while thus exposed to the unwholesome air,
But heaven, offended, may o'ertake his crime,
And, in some languishing distemper, leave him
A severe example of its violated laws.
Forbid it mercy, and forbid it love!
This may prevent it.

(Takes a steinkirk[4] from her neck and lays it gently over his head.)

And if he should wake offended at my too-busy care, let my heart-breaking patience, duty, and my fond affection plead my pardon.

[4]A French neckcloth named after the site of a French victory over the English in 1692.

Careless Vows

Marivaux
1734

Scene: a country house in France

#1—Serio-Comic
> Lucile: an independent young lady, 18

> It is decided that Lucile shall marry Damis, the son of her father's good friend. Unfortunately, the last thing headstrong young Lucile wants is to be married. She decides to write Damis a letter to this effect, and when her motives are questioned by her maid, she explains her desire to remain free of marital obligations.

LUCILE: I tell you my mind is made up, and I want you to deliver it. Do you think I pride myself on being less susceptible than other women? No, I don't make any such boast, and I would be wrong to do so—I am an affectionate soul, though rather decorous by nature and that is why marriage would be a very bad state for me. An affectionate soul has feelings, she needs them to be returned, she needs to be loved because she loves, and a person like that in the hands of a husband never gets what she needs.

[LISETTE: Lord, yes, those needs are expensive, and a husband's heart runs out of funds.]

LUCILE: I know these gentlemen a little. I notice that men are kind only when they are lovers. Their heart is the prettiest thing in the world, so long as hope keeps them in suspense. Submissive, respectful, attentive—for the little love you show them, your self-love is enchanted, it is quite delightfully served, quite surfeited with pleasure. And everything works for us—folly, arrogance, disdain, capriciousness, impertinence—everything we do is right, it's the law. We reign as tyrants, and our idolators are always on their knees. But once you marry them, once the goddess becomes human, their idolatry ends at the point where our kindness begins. As soon as they're happy, they no longer deserve to be, the ungrateful wretches!

[LISETTE: That's them!]

LUCILE: Well, I shall sort that out, and the role of goddess will not bore me, gentlemen, I can assure you! What—young and lovely as I am, I should have less than six months in a husband's eyes before my face is thrown on the scrap-heap? From being eighteen, it would suddenly jump to fifty? No, thank you very much! That would be murder. My face will only age with time, and become uglier only by lasting longer. I want my face to belong only to me, I want nobody to see what I do with it, I want it to depend only on me. If I were married, it wouldn't be *my* face any longer, it would belong to my husband—he would abandon it, it would not please him, and he would forbid it from pleasing anybody else. I would rather not have one. No, Lisette, I have no desire to be a flirt, but there are moments when your heart speaks to you and you are very glad to have your eyes free. So, no more discussion. Take my letter to Damis, and let whoever wants line up under the yoke of matrimony!

Cinna

Pierre Cornielle
1640

Scene: Ancient Rome

Dramatic

Amelia: a daughter seeking revenge for her father's death, 20s

When her father is executed by Augustus, Amelia convinces her lover and trusted member of the court, Cinna, to stage a coup. Here, she sets the scene for vengeance.

AMELIA: O restless ardor for a high revenge,
Born of a father's death, oh, child of wrath,
To which my charmèd sorrow blindly clings,
You hold too strong an empire in my heart.
Grant me some moments now when I may rest
And take account in what a state I stand,
What risks I run, what ends I would accomplish.
When I behold Augustus in his glory,
And think how, murdered by that very hand,
My father was the first step to the throne
Where now I see him; when that bloody sight,
Cause of my hate and sign of Cæsar's wrath,
Presents itself to me, then utterly
I give my soul to vengeance, and I think
How, for one death, a thousand deaths he merits
Yet even in this righteous rage, I still
Love Cinna more than I abhor Augustus,
And then I feel my fury freeze within me,
Since, slaking it, I must expose my lover.
Yes, Cinna, I am angry with myself,
Seeing the dangers into which I hurl you.
Though you are fearless in my service, still
To ask his life of you, exposes yours;
When one strikes heads from such a lofty station,
He calls upon his own a thousand tempests.
Success is doubtful, and the danger sure;
One friend disloyal can betray your plan;

One order badly planned, one chance ill-taken,
Could turn the enterprise upon its author,
Bring down on you the blow that you would strike,
And in general ruin overwhelm you.
And what your love would do for me, mischance
Might turn to your destruction. Cease, oh cease,
To risk this mortal peril; losing you
In gaining vengeance, were no gain to me.
It is too cruel a heart which can be charmed
By joys soiled by the bitterness of tears.
And one must count among the worst of evils
The death of an enemy which costs such sorrow.
But can I turn from vengeance for my father?
Is any price too dear to pay for him?
When his assassin falls beneath our hand
Should we consider what his death may cost?
Cease, vain alarms, cease, shameful tenderness,
To wring my heart to such unworthy weakness!
And you that feed them with anxiety,
Love, serve my duty, do not strive against it!
Your glory is to yield; your shame to conquer:
Show yourself noble, yielding place to duty;
The more you give, the more you shall be given,
And duty's triumph will ennoble you.

The Clandestine Marriage

George Coleman and David Garrick
1756

Scene. London

Serio-Comic

> Miss Sterling: a self-centered young lady possessed of great ambition, 18–20

The scheming Miss Sterling is about to marry Lord Melvil, a man well above her in London's caste system. Here, she wastes no time in rubbing her poor sister's nose in her new-found wealth.

MISS STERLING: Never do I desire it—never, my dear Fanny, I promise you.—Oh, how I long to be transported to the dear regions of Grosvenor Square—far—far from the dull districts of Aldersgate, Cheap, Candlewick, and Farringdon Without and Within!—My heart goes pit-a-pat at the very idea of being introduced at Court!—gilt chariot!—piebald horses!—laced liveries!—and then the whispers buzzing round the circle: "Who is that young lady? Who is she?" "Lady Melvil, ma'am!" Lady Melvil! my ears tingle at the sound.—And then at dinner, instead of my father perpetually asking: "Any news upon 'Change!" to cry: Well, Sir John! anything new from Arthur's?—or to say to some other woman of quality: Was your ladyship at the Duchess of Rubber's last night?—Did you call in at Lady Thunder's? In the immensity of crowd I swear I did not see you—Scarce a soul at the opera last Saturday.—Shall I see you at Carlisle House next Thursday?—Oh, the dear beau-monde! I was born to move in the sphere of the great world.

The Contrast

Royall Tyler
1787

Scene: New York

#1—Dramatic
    Maria: an unhappy young woman, 18–20

> Maria has been engaged to a man she neither loves nor likes by her domineering father. Here, she laments her plight and indeed the plight of all members of the "weaker" sex.

MARIA: (*A room in Van Rough's house. Maria sitting disconsolate at a table, with books, etc. Song[5].*)
The sun sets in night, and the stars shun the day;
But glory remains when their lights fade away!
Begin, ye tormentors! your threats are in vain,
For the son of Alknomook shall never complain.

Remember the arrows he shot from his bow;
No—the son of Alknomook will never complain.
Remember your chiefs by his hatchet laid low:
Why so slow?—do you wait till I shrink from the pain?

Remember the wood where in ambush we lay;
And the scalps we bore from your nation away:
Now the flame rises fast, you exult in my pain;
But the son of Alknomook can never complain.

I go to the land where my father is gone;
His ghost shall rejoice in the fame of his son:
Death comes like a friend, he relieves me from pain;
And thy son, Oh Alknomook! has scorn'd to complain.

There is something in this song which ever calls forth my affections.
The manly virtue of courage, that fortitude which steels the heart

---

[5]This popular song of the period was published in New York under the title *Alknomook* and carried the subtitle "The Death Song of the Cherokee Indians."

against the keenest misfortunes, which interweaves the laurel of glory amidst the instruments of torture and death, displays something so noble, so exalted, that in spite of the prejudices of education, I cannot but admire it, even in a savage. The prepossession which our sex is supposed to entertain for the character of a soldier is, I know, a standing piece of raillery among the wits. A cockade, a lapell'd coat, and a feather, they will tell you, are irresistable by a female heart. Let it be so.—Who is that considers the helpless situation of our sex, that does not see we each moment stand in need of a protector, and that a brave one too. Formed of the more delicate materials of nature, endowed only with softer passions, incapable, from our ignorance of the world, to guard against the wiles of mankind, our security for happiness often depends upon their generosity and courage:—Alas! how little of the former do we find. How inconsistent! that man should be leagued to destroy that honour, upon which solely rests his respect and esteem. Ten thousand temptations allure us, ten thousand passions betray us; yet the smallest deviation from the path of rectitude is followed by the contempt and insult of man, and the more remorseless pity of woman: years of penitence and tears cannot wash away the stain, nor a life of virtue obliterate its remembrance. Reputation is the life of woman; yet courage to protect it is masculine and disgusting; and the only safe asylum a woman of delicacy can find is in the arms of a man of honour. How naturally, then, should we love the brave, and the generous; how gratefully should we bless the arm raised for our protection, when nerv'd by virtue, and directed by honour! Heaven grant that the man with whom I may be connected—may be connected!—Whither has my imagination transported me—whither does it now lead me?—Am I not indissolubly engaged by every obligation of honour, which my own consent, and my father's approbation can give, to a man who can never share my affections, and whom a few days hence it will be criminal for me to disapprove—to disapprove! would to heaven that were all—to despise. For, can the most frivolous manners, actuated by the most depraved heart, meet, or merit, anything but contempt from every woman of delicacy and sentiment?

Here, Maria contemplates her filial responsibility.

MARIA: (*Alone.*) How deplorable is my situation! How distressing for a daughter to find her heart militating with her filial duty! I know my father loves me tenderly, why then do I reluctantly obey him? Heaven knows! with what reluctance I should oppose the will of a parent, or set an example of filial disobedience; at a parent's command I could wed awkwardness and deformity. Were the heart of my husband good, I would so magnify his good qualities with the eye of conjugal affection that the defects of his person and manners should be lost in the emanation of his virtues. At a father's command, I could embrace poverty. Were the poor man my husband, I would learn resignation of my lot; I would enliven our frugal meal with good humour, and chase away misfortune from our cottage with a smile. At a father's command, I could almost submit to what every female heart knows to be the most mortifying, to marry a weak man, and blush at my husband's folly in every company I visited.—But to marry a depraved wretch, whose only virtue is a polished exterior; who is actuated by the unmanly ambition of conquering the defenceless; whose heart, insensible to the emotions of patriotism, dilates at the plaudits of every unthinking girl: whose laurels are the sighs and tears of the miserable victims of his specious behaviour.—Can he, who has no regard for the peace and happiness of other families, ever have a due regard for the peace and happiness of his own? Would to heaven that my father were not so hasty in his temper! Surely, if I were to state my reasons for declining this match, he would not compel me to marry a man—whom, though my lips may solemnly promise to honour, I find my heart must ever despise.

Dione

John Gay
@1720

Scene: Arcadia

Dramatic
       Parthenia: an unhappy nymph, 18–20

    Partheni is the most beautiful nymph in Arcadia, but here she curses her appearance, for it has brought her nothing but trouble.

PARTHENIA: This melancholy scene demands a groan.
Hah! what inscription marks the weeping stone?
O pow'r of beauty! here Menalcas *lies.*
Gaze not, ye shepherds, on Parthenia's *eyes.*
Why did heav'n form me with such polished care?
Why cast my features in a mold so fair?
If blooming beauty was a blessing meant,
Why are my sighing hours deny'd content?
The downy peach, that glows with sunny dyes,
Feeds the black snail, and lures voracious flies;
The juicy pear invites the feather'd kind,
And pecking finches scoop the golden rind;
But beauty suffers more pernicious wrongs,
Blasted by envy, and censorious tongues.
How happy lives the nymph, whose comely face
And pleasing glances boast sufficient grace
To wound the swain she loves! no jealous fears
Shall vex her nuptial state with nightly tears,
Nor am'rous youths, to push their foul pretence,
Infest her days with dull impertinence.
But why talk I of love? my guarded heart
Disowns his power, and turns aside the dart.
Hark! from his hollow tomb *Menalcas* crys,
Gaze not, ye shepherds, on Parthenia's *eyes.*
Come, *Lycidas*, the mournful lay peruse,
Lest thou, like him, *Parthenia*'s eyes accuse.

The Double Inconstancy

Marivaux
1723

Scene: The Prince's palace

Dramatic
>Silvia: a young woman in love, 18–20

>The Prince has brought the beautiful young Silvia to his palace against her will for the express purpose of wooing her and making her his wife. Unfortunately for the Prince, Silvia remains true to her first love, Harlequin. Here, she lashes out at the Prince's servant.

SILVIA: Very well, servant. First: you talk about my waiting-women. They aren't waiting, they are spying and reporting on me. You steal my lover and you give me women instead; I'm *very* grateful! Any wonder that I'm sad? What do I care for concerts, music, dancing. Do you expect me to enjoy them? Harlequin's singing is better than any I've heard so far. And I can dance for myself; I'd rather; why watch other people doing it? A decent girl in a simple village has a better life than any princess weeping in her grand apartment. I didn't ask the Prince to find me attractive; I didn't try to attract him: he saw me, not the other way round; whose fault is that? He's young and kind and decent, so you say: I'm glad to hear it; let him keep all that for people as grand as him; and let him leave me with my Harlequin, who isn't a lord any more than I am a lady; who hasn't a fortune or a palace or a glorious name any more than I do; and who loves me without any style or fancy; and who is loved by me; and who I'll die of misery if I don't see soon. Oh the poor boy! What have they done to him, what has become of him? He'll be so unhappy, he'll be in despair, I know it; he's so good, so trusting! Is he being tortured? (*She moves.*)

It's horrible. Would you do me a kindness? Go away, I can't bear having you near me. Let me endure my misery in peace.

Douglas

John Home
1757

Scene: Lord Randolph's castle in the west of Scotland, 12th century

Dramatic

Lady Randolph: a melancholy widow, 30–40

Lady Randolph's first husband, Douglas, was slain in battle along with her brother. To make matters worse, their infant son was then lost in a flood. Years later, the unhappy woman has remarried and spends her days wandering her husband's estate mourning those she has lost.

LADY RANDOLPH: Ye woods and wilds, whose melancholy gloom
Accords with my soul's sadness, and draws forth
The voice of sorrow from my bursting heart,
Farewell a while: I will not leave you long;
For in your shades I deem some spirit dwells,
Who from the chiding stream, or groaning oak,
Still hears and answers to Matilda's moan.
O Douglas! Douglas! if departed ghosts
Are e'er permitted to review this world,
Within the circle of that wood thou art,
And with the passion of immortal hear'st
My lamentation: he hear'st thy wretched wife
Weep for her husband slain, her infant lost.
My brother's timeless[6] death I seem to mourn,
Who perished with thee on this fatal day.
To thee I lift my voice; to thee address
The plaint which mortal ear has never heard.
O disregard me not; though I am called
Another's now, my heart is wholly thine.
Incapable of change, affection lies
Buried, my Douglas, in thy bloody grave.—
But Randolph comes, whom fate has made my lord,
To chide my anguish, and defraud the dead.

[6]Untimely.

The Fair Penitent

Nicholas Rowe
1703

Scene: Genoa

Dramatic

> Calista: a woman driven to despair by forbidden desire, 20s

> Calista's passion for the notorious Lothario has ruined her life. Husband, father and friends have all turned from her. When the womanizing Lothario is killed in a duel, Calista keeps a lonely vigil by his body.

(The scene is a room hung with black; on one side, is Lothario's body on a bier; on the other, a table with a skull and other bones, a book, and a lamp on it. Calista is discovered on a couch in black, her hair hanging loose and disordered; after music and a song, she rises and comes forward.)

CALISTA: *(Song.)*

Hear, you midnight phantoms, hear,
You who pale and wan appear,
And fill the wretch who wakes, with fear.
You who wander, scream, and groan
'Round the mansions once your own,
You whom still your crimes upbraid,
You who rest not with the dead;
From the coverts where you stray,
Where you lurk and shun the day,
From the charnel and the tomb
Hither haste ye, hither come.

ii

Chide Calista for delay,
Tell her 'tis for her you stay;
Bid her die and come away.
See the sexton with his spade,
See the grave already made;
Listen, fair one, to thy knell,
This music is thy passing bell.
'Tis well! these solemn sounds, this pomp of horror

Are fit to feed the frenzy in my soul;
Here's room for meditation, ev'n to madness,
Till the mind burst with thinking; this dull flame
Sleeps in the socket; sure the book was left
To tell me something;—for instruction, then—
He teaches holy sorrow and contrition,
And penitence;—is it become an art then?
A trick that lazy, dull, luxurious gown-men[7]
Can teach us to do over? I'll no more on't.
(*Throwing away the book.*)
I have no more real anguish in my heart
Than all their pedant discipline e'er knew.
What charnel has been rifled for these bones?
Fie! this is pageantry;—they look uncouthly,
But what of that, if he or she that owned 'em
Safe from disquiet sit, and smile to see
The farce their miserable relics play?
But here's a sight is terrible indeed;
Is this the haughty, gallant, gay Lothario?
That dear perfidious—Ah!—how pale he looks!
How grim with clotted blood, and those dead eyes!
Ascend, ye ghosts, fantastic forms of night,
In all your diff'rent, dreadful shapes ascend,
And match the present horror if you can!

---

[7]Scholars, or, more specifically, theological scholars.

The False Servant

Marivaux
1724

Scene: a country estate in France

Dramatic
    Countess: a woman of means, 30s

The Countess here breaks off her love affair with the unscrupulous Lelio, whose jealousy is too much for her to bear.

COUNTESS: I can't contain myself. Capricious. Ridiculous. Crazy. And now, to cap it all, in bad faith. What an attractive portrait! I really didn't know you, Monsieur Lelio. I really didn't appreciate you to your full value. You've been leading me astray. So I've been making you jealous, have I? Allow me then to tell you that your jealousy is quite unbearable. It is an odious, evil jealousy which is born of a vicious, twisted mind. It has nothing to do with delicacy. It is simple an expression of those bad moods which seem to inhabit your character. That was not the kind of jealousy I was after. I was looking for that gentle doubt, which comes from an agreeable lack of self-confidence. When you are jealous in that way, may I tell you, sir, you don't go around shouting invectives at the person you love. You don't go around telling them they are ridiculous, untrustworthy and soft in the head. On the contrary. One spends one's time wondering whether one is truly loved because one has doubts as to one's merits. But you couldn't understand that. That kind of feeling is foreign to your heart. All you are acquainted with are tempers, moods and trickery. You are suspicious for no reason whatsoever. You lack respect, humility, esteem. And you build your love on a forfeit. A contract! The rights you seek to exert are repressive. A forfeit, Monsieur Lelio! Suspicions and a forfeit! Is that love? If it is, it's a kind of love which gives me shivers down the spine. Farewell.

Fatal Curiosity

George Lillo
1737

Scene: Penryn in Cornwall

#1—Dramatic
> Charlot: a young woman whose fiancé has been missing for seven years, 20–30

Charlot has waited patiently for seven years for the missing Wilmot to return from India. When a friend suggests that she get on with her life, she replies that she intends to stand by the promise she made to Wilmot to love only him.

CHARLOT: I'll not despair
(Patience shall cherish hope), nor wrong his honor
By unjust suspicion. I know his truth,
And will preserve my own. But to prevent
All future vain, officious importunity,
Know, thou incessant foe of my repose,
Whether he sleeps secure from mortal cares
In the deep bosom of the boist'rous main,
Or, tossed with tempests, still endures it rage;
Whether his weary pilgrimage by land
Has found an end and he now rests in peace
In earth's cold womb, or wanders o'er her face;
Be it my lot to waste, in pining grief,
The remnant of my days for his known loss
Or live, as now, uncertain and in doubt,
No second choice shall violate my vows.
High Heaven, which heard them and abhors the perjured,
Can witness they were made without reserve,
Never to be retracted, ne'er dissolved
By accidents or absence, time or death!

Agnes, a woman made desperate by poverty, 40–50

Years of hard living have left their mark on Agnes. When a mysterious stranger, who is really her long-lost son in disguise, gives her a small casket to look after, curiosity compels her to open it. When she beholds the jewels inside, Agnes knows with sudden certainty that she'd rather kill than surrender them.

AGNES: (*Alone, with the casket in her hand.*)
Who should this stranger be? And then this casket—
He says it is of value, and yet trusts it,
As if a trifle, to a stranger's hand.
His confidence amazes me. Perhaps
It is not what he says. I'm strongly tempted
To open it and see. No, let it rest.
Why should my curiosity excite me
To search and pry into th'affairs of others,
Who have t'employ my thoughts so many cares
And sorrows of my own?—With how much ease
The spring gives way!—Surprising! most prodigious!
My eyes are dazzled and my ravished heart
Leaps at the glorious sight. How bright's the luster,
How immense the worth of these fair jewels!
Aye, such a treasure would expel forever
Base poverty and all its abject train:
The mean devices we're reduced to use
To keep out famine and preserve our lives
From day to day, the cold neglect of friends,
The galling scorn or more provoking pity
Of an insulting world. Possessed of these,
Plenty, content, and power might take their turn,
And lofty pride bare its aspiring head
At our approach and once more bend before us.
A pleasing dream!—'Tis past, and now I wake
More wretched by the happiness I've lost.
For sure it was a happiness to think,
Though but a moment, such a treasure mine.
Nay, it was more than I thought. I saw and touched
The bright temptation, and I see it yet.

'Tis here—'tis mine—I have it in possession!
Must I resign it? Must I give it back?
Am I in love with misery and want,
To rob myself and court so vast a loss?
Retain it, then! But how? There is a way—
Why sinks my heart? Why does my blood run cold?
Why am I thrilled with horror? 'Tis not choice,
But dire necessity, suggests the thought!

The Fatal Friendship

Catherine Trotter
1698

Scene: England

Dramatic
> Lamira: a wealthy widow, 20–30

> Lamira is in love with Gramont. Not knowing of his secret marriage to Felicia, she forces Gramont to marry her by holding her wealth as a carrot to his greedy father. When the unhappy Gramont refuses to touch her on their wedding night, she confronts him angrily.

LAMIRA: Oh, could I be convinced of that, Gramont,
I should not envy the most unhappy bride.
I have no thought, no wish beyond your love;
Make me secure of that, and I am blest.
Why art thou thus unmoved, thou cruel savage?
Hast thou no sensibility, no fire in thy soul?
Or have not I the art to blow the flame?
Instruct me then, if 'tis not yet too late,
If 'tis not kindled at another's charms.
That was an injurious thought, chide it away,
Tell me you could not be so false, so base.
You do not answer!
Nay, then I fear I am abused indeed.
Speak quickly, swear I am not, the very fear's
Distracting, not to be borne, swear you are thus by nature,
Thus cold, insensible to all the sex
As you are now to me, swear that,
And I'll complain no more of your indifference,
But with submissive duty, tenderest care,
And most unwearied love, still strive to move
Thy cold, obdurate heart. Is there a hope to gain it?
[*GRAMONT:* Madam, you set it at too high a rate,
It is not worth your least concern or thought.]
LAMIRA: Why, why inhuman dost thou answer thus,
Regardless of the doubts that rack my soul?
Oh speak, reply to them, e'er they distract me.

'Tis enough, enough. Thy silence speaks
The dumb confession of a guilty mind.
Ay, there it is, thou false, perfidious man!
'Tis to a rival I am sacrificed.
But think'st thou I will tamely bear my wrongs,
And let her triumph in 'em? Dare not to see her,
For, if thou dost, I'll find the strumpet out.
Confusion! Slighted, for another, too!
Oh, how I'll be revenged! I'll know this scorceress,
Make her most infamous,
I'll be your plague, anticipate your hell!

Jeppe of the Hill
Ludvig Holberg
1723

Scene: a village in Denmark

Serio-Comic
> Nille: the disgruntled wife of a lazy man, 30s

Here, shrewish Nille complains of Jeppe's slothful ways.

NILLE: (*Alone.*) I don't think there's a lazier scoundrel in the whole country than my husband! I can hardly wake him up when I pull him out of his bed by his hair. That scoundrel knows today is market day, and still, he sleeps so long. Just the other day Parson Poul, said to me, "Nille, you're too hard on your husband, after all, he is and should be master of the house." But I answered, "No, my good Mr. Poul, if I let my husband rule this house for just one year, neither the baron would get his rent nor the parson his offerings, for in that time he'd drink up everything in the house! Should I let a man be master of the house when he's ready to sell his furniture, wife, children, and even himself for brandy?" At that, Parson Poul became very quiet and wiped his hand across his mouth. The overseer agrees with me and says, "My dear woman, ignore what the parson says. It does say in the ritual that you should honor and obey your husband; but on the other hand, it's written in your lease, which is more current than your vows, that you must keep up your farm and pay your rent, which for you is impossible unless you drag your husband out of bed every day by the hair and beat him to work." I just pulled him out of bed and went out to the barn to see how the work was going; when I went back in he was sitting on the chair, sound asleep, with his pants, to be polite, on just one leg. Well I grabbed my switch down from the hook and licked my good Jeppe until he was wide awake again. The only thing he's afraid of is Master Erich; that's what I call my switch.[8] Hey, Jeppe! Is your ass covered yet? Do you want to talk to Master Erich again? Hey Jeppe, get out here!

---

[8]Nille's switch is a braided leather whip.

A Journey to London

Sir John Vanbrugh
1728

Serio-Comic

Lady Arabella: a disgruntled wife, 20–30

When a younger friend suggests that married people must become so familiar to one another that they have to struggle to make conversation, Arabella hastens to assure her that married people find things to talk about that single folk could never imagine.

LADY ARABELLA: Clarinda, you are the most mistaken in the world; marry'd People have things to talk of, Child, that never enter into the Imagination of others. Why now, here's my Lord and I, we han't been marry'd above two short Years you know, and we have already eight or ten Things constantly in Bank, that whenever we want Company, we can talk of any one of them for two Hours together, and the Subject never the flatter. It will be as fresh next Day, if we have occasion for it, as it was the first Day it entertain'd us.

[*CLARINDA:* Why that must be wonderful pretty.]

LADY ARABELLA: O there's noLife like it. This very Day now for Example, my Lord and I, after a pretty cheerful *tête à tête* Dinner, sat down by the Fire-side, in an idle, indolent, pick-tooth Way for a while, as if we had not thought of another's being in the Room. At last (stretching himself, and yawning twice) My Dear, says he, you came home very late last Night. 'Twas but Two in the Morning, says I. I was in bed (yawning) by Eleven, says he. So you are every Night, says I. Well, says he, I am amazed, how you can sit up so late. How can you be amazed, says I, at a Thing that happens so often? Upon which, we enter'd into Conversation. And tho', this is a Point has entertain'd us above fifty times already, we always find so many pretty new Things to say upon't that I believe in my Soul it will last as long as we live.

The Lancashire Witches

Thomas Shadwell
1682

Scene: England

Serio-Comic
    Mrs. Dickenson: a witch, any age.

  Here, a nasty Witch tells of a recent adventure.

DICKENSON: From the Seas slimy owse a Weed
I fetch'd to open Locks at need.
With Coats tuck'd up, and with my Hair,
All flowing loosely in the Air,
With naked Feet I went among
The poysonous Plants, there Adders Tongue,
With Aconite and Martagon,
Henbane, Hemlock, Moon-wort too,
Wild Fig-Tree, that o're Tombs do's grow,
The deadly Night-shade, Cypress, Yew,
And Libbards Bane, and venomous Dew,
I gathered for my Charms. *Harg*. And I
Dug up a Mandrake which did cry.
Three Circles I made, and the Wind was good,
And looking to the West I stood.

The Learned Women

Molière

1672

Scene: Paris

Serio-Comic

      Armande: a young lady obsessed with learning, 18–20

    Clitandre once courted Armande but soon tired of her esoteric prattle. He then transferred his affections to Armande's younger sister, whom he now plans to marry. Enraged, Armande insists that the union not be permitted. This eventually leads to a confrontation between Armande and Clitandre in which she reviles her former beau for his physical lust.

ARMANDE: Do I oppose the wishes of your heart
When I seek to root out their vulgar part,
And ask a purity in your desires
Consistent with what perfect love requires?
You couldn't school your thoughts to abstinence,
For me, from the degrading claims of sense?
And you've no taste for the serene delight
Felt when two disembodied hearts unite?
You can live only in this brutish wise?
Only with all the train of fleshly ties?
And to nourish the fires produced in you
You must have marriage, and what follows too?
Oh, what a strange love! Hear me, if you please:
Noble souls burn with no such flame as these!
In all their glow the senses have no part,
And all they seek to marry is the heart;
With scorn they leave aside other desires.
Their flames are pure, like the celestial fires.
Their love gives vent only to virtuous sighs,
And crass desires they utterly despise.
Nothing impure contaminates their goals;
They love for love alone, a love of souls;
Their transports are directed to the mind;
The body is ignored and left behind.

The Libertine

Thomas Shadwell

1676

Scene: Spain

Dramatic

Maria: a woman abused by Don Juan, 20–30

Maria has given up everything to follow Don Juan in a mad pursuit of vengeance. Here, she reveals her hatred for the infamous libertine as well as for the entire male race.

MARIA: (*In man's habit, enter Maria and her maid Flora.*) Thus I have
abandoned all my Fortune, and laid by My Sex.
Revenge for thee. Assist me now,
You Instruments of Bloud, for my dear Brothers,
And for my much more dear *Octavio*'s sake.
Where are my Bravo's?—
[*FLORA:* Thay have beset the Villains House,
And he shall ne'r come out alive.—]
MARIA: O let 'em shew no more remorse,
Than Hungry Lions o'r their prey will.
How miserable am I made by that
Inhumane Monster! No savage Beast,
Wild deserts e'r brought forth, provoked
By all its hunger, and its natural rage,
Could yet have been so cruel.
Oh my *Octavio!* whether thou art fled,
From the most loving and most wretched
Creature of her Sex? What Ages of delight
Each hour with thee brought forth!
How much, when I had thee, was all the world
Unenvied by me! Nay, I piti'd all my Sex,
That cou'd have nothing worth their care,
Since all the treasure of Mankind was mine.
Methought I cou'd look down on Queens, when he
Was with me: but now, compared to me,
How happy is the Wretched, whose sinews

Crack upon the merciless Engine
Of his torture? I live with greater torments then he dies.
[*FLORA:* Leave your complaints. Tears are no Sacrifice for bloud.]
MARIA: Now my just grief to just revenge give place
I am ashamed of these soft Tears, till I've
Revenged thy horrid Murder, Oh that I could
Make the Villain linger out an Age in
Torments! But I will revel in his bloud: Oh
I could suck the last drop that warms the
Monsters heart, that might inspire me with
Such cruelty, as vile Man, with all his horrid
Arts of power, is yet a stranger to;
Then I might root out all his cursed Race.

The London Merchant or
The History of George Barnwell
George Lillo
1731

Scene: London

Serio-Comic
    Millwood: a scheming woman, 30s

> Millwood is an unscrupulous woman who preys on younger men. Here she awaits
> the arrival of her latest victim.

MILLWOOD: It's a general maxim among the knowing part of
mankind, that a woman without virtue, like a man without honour or
honesty, is capable of any action, though never so vile; and yet what
pains will they not take, what arts not use, to seduce us from our innocence, and make us contemptible and wicked, even in their own opin-
ions! Then is it not just, the villains, to their cost, should find us so? But
guilt makes them suspicious, and keeps them on their guard; therefore
we can take advantage only of the young and innocent part of the sex,
who, having never injured women, apprehend no injury from them.
[*LUCY:* Ay, they must be young indeed.]
MILLWOOD: Such a one, I think, I have found. As I've passed through
the City, I have often observed him, receiving and paying considerable
sums of money; from thence I conclude he is employed in affairs of
consequence.
[*LUCY:* Is he handsome?]
MILLWOOD: Ay, ay, the stripling is well made and has a good face.
[*LUCY:* About—
MILLWOOD: Eighteen.
[*LUCY:* Innocent, handsome, and about eighteen! You'll be vastly
happy. Why, if you manage well, you may keep him to yourself these
two or three years.]
MILLWOOD: If I manage well, I shall have done with him much
sooner. Having long had a design on him, and meeting him yesterday, I
made a full stop, and, gazing wishfully on his face, asked him his name.
He blushed, and bowing very low, answered: "George Barnwell." I

begged his pardon for the freedom I had taken, and told him he was the person I had long wished to see, and to whom I had an affair of importance to communicate at a proper time and place. He named a tavern; I talked of honour and reputation, and invited him to my house. He swallowed the bait, promised to come, and this is the time I expect him. (*Knocking at the door.*) Somebody knocks;—d'ye hear; I am at home to nobody to-day but him. (*Exit Lucy.*)—Less affairs must give way to those of more consequence, and I am strangely mistaken if this does not prove of great importance to me and him too, before I have done with him. Now, after what manner shall I receive him? Let me consider— what manner of person am I to receive? He is young, innocent, and bashful: therefore I must take care not to put him out of countenance at first. But then, if I have any skill in physiognomy, he is amorous, and, with a little assistance, will soon get the better of his modesty. I'll e'en trust to Nature, who does wonders in these matters. If I seem what one is not, in order to be better liked for what one really is; if to speak one thing, and mean the direct contrary, be art in a woman—I know nothing of nature.

Love in a Village

Isaac Bickerstaff
1763

Scene: a village

Serio-Comic
Mrs. Woodcock: a concerned Aunt, 40–50

Mrs. Woodcock has discovered that her niece has planned to elope with her music teacher. Here, she sets the impulsive young woman straight.

MRS. DEB: This is mighty pretty romantic stuff! but you learn it out of your play-books and novels. Girls in my time had other employments; we worked at our needles, and kept ourselves from idle thoughts: before I was your age, I had finished, with my own fingers, a complete set of chairs, and a fire-screen in ten-stitch; four counterpanes in Marseilles quilting; and the Creed and Ten Commandments, in the hair of our family: it was fram'd and glaz'd, and hung over the parlour chimney-piece, and your poor dear grandfather was prouder of it than e'er a picture in his house. I never looked into a book, but when I said my prayers, except it was the Complete Housewife, or the great family receipt-book: whereas you are always at your studies! Ah, I never knew a woman come to good, that was fond of reading.

Love Letters to a Gentleman

Aphra Behn
1696

Scene: London

Serio-Comic

Astrea: a young woman in love, 20s

After a strange courtship consisting of many letters passed back and forth, Astrea here boldly confesses her love for Lycidas in yet another letter.

ASTREA: My charming unkind,

I would have engaged my life you could not have left me so coldly, so unconcerned as you did; but you are resolved to give me proofs of your no love. Your counsel, which was given you tonight, has wrought the effects which it usually does in hearts like yours. Tell me no more you love me; for 'twill be hard to make me think it, though it be the only blessing I ask on earth. But if love can merit a heart, I know who ought to claim yours. My soul is ready to burst with pride and indignation; and at the same time, love, with all his softness assails me, and will make me write: so that between one and the other, I can express neither as I ought. What shall I do to make you know I do not use to condescend to so much submission, nor to tell my heart so freely? Though you think it use, methinks, I find my heart swell with disdain at this minute, for my being ready to make asseverations of the contrary, and to assure you I do not, nor never did love, or talk at the rate I do to you, since I was born. I say, I would swear this, but something rolls up my bosom, and checks my very thought as it rises. You ought, oh faithless, and infinitely adorable Lycidas! to know and guess my tenderness; you ought to see it grow, and daily increase upon your hands. If it be troublesome, 'tis because I fancy you lessen, whilst I increase, in passion; or rather, that by your ill judgment of mine, you never had any in your soul for me. Oh unlucky, oh vexatious thought! Either let me never see that charming face, or ease my soul of so tormenting an agony, as the cruel thought of not being beloved. Why, my lovely dear, should I flatter you? or, why make more words of my tenderness, than another woman, that loves as well, would do, as once you said? No, you ought rather to believe that I say more, because I have more than any woman can be capable of. My soul is formed of no other material than love; and all that soul of love was formed for my dear, faithless Lycidas—methinks I have a fancy, that something will prevent my going tomorrow morning. However, I conjure thee, if possible, to come tomorrow about seven or eight at night, that I may tell you in what a deplorable condition you left me tonight. I cannot describe it; but I feel it, and with you the same pain, for going so inhumanely. But oh! you went to joys, and left me to torments! You went to love alone, and left me love and rage, fevers and calentures,[9] even madness itself! Indeed, indeed, my soul! I know not to what degree I love you; let it suffice I do most passionately, and can have no thoughts of any other man, whilst I have life. No! Reproach me, defame me, lampoon me, curse me, and kill me, when I do, and let Heaven do so too.

Farewell—I love you more and more every moment of my life. Know it, and goodnight. Come tomorrow, being Wednesday, to, my adorable Lycidas, your
Astrea.

---

[9] A tropical fever once thought to be caused by the heat.

The Misanthrope

Molière
1666

Scene: Paris

#1—Serio-Comic
Arsinoé: a woman with a tendency to gossip, 20s

Bitchy Arsinoé here pays a visit to her friend, Célimène, for the express purpose of "warning" her about the unsavory things being said about her recent behavior.

ARSINOÉ: There's something that I think I ought to say.
[CÉLIMÈNE: Just seeing you makes this a perfect day.]
(Exit Acaste and Clitandre, laughing.)
ARSINOÉ: Their leaving now was apropos indeed.
[CÉLIMÈNE: Shall we sit down?]
ARSINOÉ: I do not see the need,
Madame. True friendship should be manifest
In subjects that concern our interest;
And since none matter more to you or me
Than those of honor and propriety,
I come to tell you something, as a friend,
On which your reputation may depend.
I spent the other day with virtuous folk,
And, as it happened, 'twas of you they spoke.
And there, Madame, the freedom of your ways
Had the misfortune not to meet with praise.
The many men from whom you seek applause,
The rumors your coquettish manners cause,
Found far more censors than they ever ought,
And harsher than I could have wished or thought.
On this, you can imagine where I stood:
I sprang to your defense—as best I could,
Excusing your behavior as well-meant,
And stating I would vouch for your intent.
But there are things, you know as well as I,
We can't excuse, however hard we try;
And so I had to grant the other's claim

That your behavior does not help your name,
That it affords you anything but glory,
And makes of you the butt of many a story,
And that your ways, if you amended them,
Might offer less occasion to condemn.
Not that I think you grant more than you ought:
Heaven preserve my mind from such a thought!
But people hanker so for signs of vice,
To live well for oneself does not suffice.
Madame, I think you have too wise a heart
Not to accept this counsel in good part,
And to suspect a motive in my breast
Other than fervor for your interest.

#2—Serio-Comic
        Célimène: a self-assured young woman with many suitors, 20s

    Here, Célimène repays Arsinoé's advice with a few choice words of her own.

CÉLIMÈNE: Madame, do not misjudge my attitude:
Advice like yours is cause for gratitude;
Now let me show my deep appreciation
By counsel that deserves your reputation,
And since I see you show your amity
By telling me what people say of me,
I'll take your kind example as my cue,
And let you know the things they say of you.
I visited some friends the other day—
People of merit—and it chanced that they
Sought to define the art of living well.
On you, Madame, the conversation fell.
Your prudery, your ready indignation
Were not, alas! held up for admiration.
That affectation of a pious face,
Eternal talk of honor and of grace,
Your screams and airs of outraged innocence,
When a harmless word allows a doubtful sense,
The self-esteem that gratifies your mind,
The pitying eye you cast upon mankind,

44

Your frequent lessons, and the wrath you vent
On matters that are pure and innocent:
All this, to speak without equivocation,
Madame, gives rise to general condemnation.
"Why does she wear," they said, "this modest guise,
This pious mask which all the rest belies?
Though she would never miss a time to pray,
She beats her servants and withholds their pay.
In church she flaunts her zealous sense of duty,
Yet paints her face and strives to be a beauty.
She covers up the nude when it's in paint,
But of the thing itself makes no complaint."
Against them all I spoke right up for you,
Assuring them that none of this was true;
Still nothing would they do but criticize,
And they concluded that you would be wise
To leave the acts of others more alone,
And think a little more about your own;
That we should take an earnest look within
Before we censure other people's sin;
That only those whose lives approach perfection
Are licensed to administer correction;
And that we leave this better, even then,
To those whom Heaven has chosen among men.
Madame, you too have far too wise a heart
No to accept this counsel in good part,
And to suspect a motive in my breast
Other than a fervor for your interest.

The Mischievous
Machinations of Scapin
Molière
1671

Scene: Naples

Serio-Comic
> Zerbinette: a young woman born to a wealthy family captured and raised by gypsies, 18–20

> Zerbinette has fallen in love with the son of an infamous miser. Following many misadventures, she unwittingly tells the tale to Géronte, the miser in question.

ZERBINETTE: This has nothing to do with you, and I'm laughing to myself at a story I've just been told, the funniest you ever heard. I don't know whether it's because I'm involved in the thing; But I've never come across anything as funny as a trick that has just been played by a son on his father to get some money out of him.

[*GÉRONTE:* By a son on his father, to get some money out of him?]

ZERBINETTE: Yes. With the least bit of urging, you'll find me willing enough to tell you all about it, and I've a natural itch to communicate the stories I know.

[*GÉRONTE:* Pray tell me this story.]

ZERBINETTE: I'm willing. I won't risk very much by telling it to you, and it's an adventure that's not likely to be secret long. Destiny willed that I find myself among a band of these people who are called Gypsies and who, roaming from province to province, involve themselves in telling fortunes, and sometimes in many other things. When we arrived in this town, a young man saw me and fell in love with me. From that moment on he has followed me around, and at first he was like all these young fellows, who think all they have to do is speak and that at the slightest word they say to us their business is done; but he found a pride that made him correct his original ideas a little. He made his passion known to the people whose hands I was in, and he found them disposed to give me up to him in consideration for a certain sum. But the trouble with the business was that my suitor found himself in the state in which we very often see most young men of good condition, that is to say that he was a bit bare of money, and he has a father who, though rich, is an arrant skinflint, the meanest man in the world. Wait!.

Can't I even remember his name? Hey! Help me a little. Can't you tell me the name of someone in this town who is known for being a miser to the highest degree?

[*GÉRONTE:* No]

ZERBINETTE: There's a *ron* in his name, *ronte*. Or . . . *Oronté*. No. *Gé* . . . *Géronte;* yes, Géronte, that's just it; that's my miser, I've got it, that's the skinflint I'm talking about. To come to our story, today our people wanted to leave this town and my sweetheart was going to lose me for want of money. So, in order to get some out of his father, he hadn't found help in the ingenuity of a servant he has. As for the servant's name, I know it perfectly; his name is Scapin; he's an incomparable man, and he deserves all the praise that can be given.

[*GÉRONTE:* (*Aside.*) Ah! You scoundrel!]

ZERBINETTE: Here's the stratagem he used to catch his dupe. Ha, ha, ha, ha! I can't think back on it without laughing with all my heart. Ha, ha, ha! He went and found this dog of a miser, ha, ha, ha! and told him that he was walking in the port with his son, he, hee! they had seen a Turkish galley and been invited to go aboard; that a young Turk had given them a collation, ha! that while they were eating, the galley had put out to sea; and that the Turk had sent him back to land, alone, in a skiff, with orders to tell his master's father that he was taking his son to Algiers unless he sent him five hundred crowns right away. Ha, ha, ha! There is my skinflint, my miser in frenzied anguish; and the tenderness he has for his son puts on a weird combat with his avarice. Five hundred crowns that they demand of him are precisely five hundred dagger thrusts. Ha, ha, ha! He can't bring himself to tear this sum from his entrails; and the pain he suffers makes him find a hundred ridiculous ways of getting his son back. Ha, ha, ha! He wants to send the police to sea after the Turk's galley. Ha, ha, ha! He solicits his valet to go and offer himself in his son's place until he has raised the money that he doesn't want to give. Ha, ha, ha! To make up the five hundred crowns, he gives up four or five old suits that aren't worth thirty. Ha, ha, ha! The valet makes him understand, at every turn, the pointlessness of his propositions, and each reflection is lugubriously accompanied by a "But what the devil did he go into that galley for? Ah! Cursed galley! Traitor of a Turk!" Finally, after many evasions, after long having groaned and sighed. . . . But it seems to me that you're not laughing at my story? What do you think of it?

Phèdre

Jean Racine
1677

Scene: Trezene: a city in the Pelopannesos

#1—Dramatic
> Aricie: a captive princess, 18–20

> Here, Aricie confesses her love for Hippolyte, the son of Theseus, her captor.

ARICIE: I listen, dear Ismène, my heart in all its youth
devours what you say, although there's not much truth!
You who are dear to me, you know my great distress:
my heart has only known my own soul's loneliness,
I who have been the toy of accident and chance,
how can I know the joy, the folly of romance?
The daughter of a King from this great ancient shore,
I only have survived the tragedies of war.
I lost six brothers who were strong and brave and free,
the hope and flower of a famous family!
The sword tore all of them, the earth was wet with red,
Erectheus was dead when all these sons had bled.
You know that since their death, there was a stern decree
forbidding any Greek to fall in love with me:
the flame of my desire might kindle in my womb,
and one day light a fire within my brother's tomb.
Besides, you ought to know with what a haughty frown
I viewed this conqueror and what he had set down.
For I had hated love through my disdainful days,
and so I thanked Theseus, and even gave him praise
for making me obey the vows I had begun.
But then I had not seen this fearless hero's son.
Not that my eyes alone were held by his fair face,
and made to dwell upon his celebrated grace—
those gifts which nature gives, which anyone would prize,
he seems to set aside, as something to despise.
I love and value him for what makes him unique:
his father's deeds, and not the ways that he was weak:

I love, and I admire the scope of his high pride,
which never yet was tamed, has never yet been tied.
How Phèdre was taken in by Theseus and his sighs!
I have more self-respect, and my affection flies
from all these easy vows passed out to everyone:
such offers leave me cold, they're something that I shun.
To teach humility to the inflexible,
to speak of suffering to the insensible,
to chain a prisoner with claims that I would make,
which he could strain against, but never really break—
that is what I desire, that will make me complete;
and yet strong Hercules fought less than Hippolyte;
subdued more often, and seduced more easily,
he gave less glory to each lover he would see.
But dear Ismène, alas!—what awful things I dare!
I will come up against more force than I can bear.
Perhaps you may hear me, humble in my despair,
groan under that high pride which now I think so fair.
Hippolyte fall in love?—how could my hope or fear
affect him in the least . . .

#2—Dramatic
          Phèdre: unhappy wife of Theseus, 30s

    Believing Theseus to be dead, Phèdre finally feels free to confess her love for his son,
    Hippolyte. When she does so, the young man recoils in horror, for his heart belongs
    to Aricie. Enraged, Phèdre dares him to strike her down.

PHÈDRE: You understood too well. O cruelty!
I must have said enough to make it all quite clear.
Well then, prepare to see Phèdre in her fury here.
I am in love. And yet, seeing this sentiment,
do not believe I think that I am innocent,
or that the passion which is poisoning my mind
has been encouraged by complacence of some kind.
I am the sick victim of the spite of the skies;
I mightily despise myself in my own eyes.
The gods are my witness, the same great gods who lit
a fire in my blood and then kept fanning it;

these gods who take their delight in their deceit and seek
to seduce and undo a woman who is weak.
Now you yourself know well what happened in the past:
I chased you from this place and made you an outcast.
I tried to show myself so odious to you,
by being hateful and inhuman in your view.
What good was this great war I waged without success?
You hated me much more, I did not love you less.
Your sadness gave your face a charm beyond your years.
I languished, I burned up, in fire and in tears.
Your eyes could witness to the truth of what I say,
if you could lift them up and make them look my way.
What am I saying now?—have I become so ill
I could make such a vow, and of my own free will?
I fear for my one son, I must protect this child,
and so I had begun to ask you to be mild.
The feeble weakness of a heart too full to speak!
Alas, for it is you and you alone I seek.
Revenge yourself, my Lord, on my disgraceful shame.
Son of a hero who first gave you your own name,
here is your chance to kill another beast of Crete:
the wife of Theseus dares to love Hippolyte!
This terrible monster should not escape you now.
Here is my heart, right here, it's waiting for your blow.
It is impatient now to pay for its foul lust,
it feels your hand reach out and make the fatal thrust.
So strike. Or if you think your hatred should abstain
from granting me at least this last sweet peaceful pain,
or if you think my blood would soil your hand, my Lord,
then do not make a move, yet let me have your sword.
Now.

When Phèdre discovers that her husband is still alive, she realizes that her life is over and laments her unhappy fate.

PHÈDRE: They will love forever.
And right now, as I speak—ah! what a deadly thought!—
they brave the rage of one who raves and is distraught.
Despite the long exile which takes them far apart,
they swear they will remain within each other's heart.
No, no, Oenone, no, no, I cannot bear their joy;
take pity on my hate which hastens to destroy.
This Aricie must die. My husband must revive
his wrath against that race he said must not survive.
And he must not lay down a few light penalties:
this sister has surpassed her brother's blasphemies.
My jealousy will speak and seek ways to cajole.
What am I doing now? have I lost all control?
I, jealous! and Theseus becomes the one I seek!
My husband is alive, and love still makes me weak!
For whom? and for whose heart are all my prayers addressed?
Each word I say creates new chaos in my breast.
Now all my hopes fly off beyond all scope of crime.
Incest and fraud exist in me at the same time.
My own cold reckless hands, restless for violence,
are burning to disturb the breath of innocence.
Wretched! and I still live? I am still in the sight
of that great sacred sun which bore me in its light?
My father is the first of all the gods on high;
and my own ancestors still populate the sky.
Where can I hide! far down in the foul dark of hell.
But how? for even there my father casts a spell;
he holds the fatal urn the gods put in his hand:
Minos dooms all who fall to that last ghastly land.
Ah, just imagine how his spirit will
despair when his own daughter comes into his presence there,
confessing all her crimes, with shame in every word,
and sins the underworld perhaps has never heard!

Father, what will you say when I have said it all?
I know, your hand will drop, the fatal urn will fall;
then you shall have to choose what torment you prefer,
so you yourself can be my executioner.
Forgive me: a cruel god has damned this family;
and he still takes revenge in my anxiety.
Alas! and my sad heart has never known the taste
of this forbidden love for which I am disgraced.
Pursued by suffering until my dying breath,
I leave a painful life as I fly towards my death.

Pizarro

Richard Brinsley Sheridan
1799

Scene: Peru

Dramatic

Cora: a young mother searching for her husband, 20s

Cora's husband, Alonzo, has deserted Pizarro's ranks because he became disgusted by the brutality of the Spanish against the Incans. Following a bloody battle, Cora is told that Alonzo has been taken prisoner by Pizarro. Here, she vows to march into Pizarro's camp and find her husband.

CORA: Ha! does my reason fail me, or what is this horrid light that presses on my brain? Oh, Alonzo! It may be that thou hast fallen victim to thy own guileless heart—hadst thou been silent, hadst thou not made a fatal legacy of these wretched charms—
[*ROLLA:* Cora! what hateful suspicion has possessed thy mind?]
CORA: Yes, yes, 'tis clear—his spirit was ensnar'd; he was led to the fatal spot, where mortal valour could not front a host of murderers—He fell—in vain did he exclaim for help to Rolla. At a distance you look'd on and smil'd—You could have saved him—could—but did not.
[*ROLLA:* Oh, glorious sun! can I have deserved this? Cora, rather bid me strike this sword into my heart.]
CORA: No! live! live for love! for that love thou seekest; whose blossoms are to shoot from the bleeding grave of thy betray'd and slaughter'd friend!—But thou hast borne to me the *last words* of my *Alonzo!* Now hear *mine*—Sooner shall this boy draw poison from this tortured breast—sooner would I link me to the pallid corse of the meanest wretch that perish'd with Alonzo, than he call Rolla father—than I call Rolla husband!
[*ROLLA:* Yet call me what I am—thy friend, thy protector!]
CORA: (Distractedly.) Away! I have no protector but my God!—With this child in my arms will I hasten to the field of slaughter—There with these hands will I turn up to the light every mangled body—seeking, howe'er by death disfigur'd, the sweet smile of my Alonzo:—with fearful cries I will shriek out his name till my veins snap! If the smallest spark of life remains, he will know the voice of his Cora, open for a moment his unshrouded eyes, and bless me with a last look: But if we find

him not—Oh! then, my boy, we will to the Spanish camp—that look of thine will win me passage through a thousand swords—They too are men.—Is there a heart that could drive back the wife that seeks her bleeding husband; or the innocent babe that cries for his imprison'd father? No, no, my child, every where we shall be safe.—A wretched mother bearing a poor orphan in her arms, has Nature's passport through the world. Yes, yes, my son, we'll go and seek thy father.

Polly Honeycombe

George Coleman
1760

Scene: London

Serio-Comic
Polly: a romantic young woman, 16–18

Here, Polly takes a great delight in reading a cheap romance novel out loud.

POLLY: Well said, Sir George!—O the dear man!—But so—'With the words the enraptured baronet (*Reading.*) concluded his declaration of love.'—So!—'But what heart can imagine, (*Reading.*) what tongue describe, or what pen delineate, the amiable confusion of Emilia?'—Well! Now for it!—'Reader, if thou art a courtly reader, thou hast seen at polite tables, iced cream crimsoned with raspberries; or, if thou art an uncourtly reader, thou hast seen the rosy-fingered morning, dawning in the golden east';—Dawning in the golden east!—Very pretty!—'Thou hast seen, perhaps, (*Reading.*) the artificial vermilion on the cheeks of Cleora, or the vermilion of nature on those of Sylvia; thou hast seen—in a word, the lovely face of Emilia was overspread with blushes '—This is a most beautiful passage, I protest! Well, a novel for my money! Lord, lord, my stupid papa has no taste. He has no notion of humour, and character, and the sensibility of delicate feeling. (*Affectedly.*) And then mama,—but where was I?—Oh here—'Overspread with blushes. (*Reading.*) Sir George, touched at her confusion, gently seized her hand, and softly pressing it to his bosom, (*Acting it as she reads.*) where the pulses of his heart beat quick, throbbing with tumultuous passion, in a plaintive tone of voice breathed out, 'Will you not answer me, Emilia?'''—Tender creature!—'She, half raising (*Reading and acting.*) her downcast eyes, and half inclining her averted head, said in faltering accents—'Yes, Sir!'''—Well, now!—'Then gradually recovering with ineffable sweetness she prepared to address him; when Mrs. Jenkinson bounced into the room, threw down a set of china in her hurry, and strewed the floor with porcelain fragments: then turning Emilia round and round, whirled her out of the apartment in an instant, and struck Sir George dumb with astonishment at her appearance. She raved; but the baronet resumed his accustomed effrontery—'

The Prince of Parthia

Thomas Godfrey

1767

Scene: Ctesiphon

#1—Dramatic

> Queen: a woman driven to treachery by hatred and jealousy, 40s

> When the Queen discovers that her husband has fallen in love with the beautiful young Evanthe, she flies into a dark rage. The first part of her revenge is to turn one of their sons against the other as she here confesses to her maid.

QUEEN: Soft is thy nature, but alas! *Edessa*,
Thy heart's a stranger to a mother's sorrows,
To see the pride of all her wishes blasted,
Thy fancy cannot paint the storm of grief,
Despair and anguish, which my breast has known.
Oh! shower, ye Gods, your torments on *Arsaces*,
Curs'd be the morn which dawned upon his birth.
[*EDESSA:* Yet, I intreat—]
QUEEN: Away! for I will curse—
O may he never know a father's fondness,
Or know it to his sorrow, may his hopes
Of joy be cut like mine, and his short life
Be one continu'd tempest: if he lives,
Let him be curs'd with jealousy and fear,
And vext with anguish of neglecting scorn;
May tort'ring hope present the flowing cup,
Then hasty snatch it from his eager thirst,
And when he dies base treach'ry be the means.
[*EDESSA:* Oh! calm your spirits.]
QUEEN: Yes, I'll now be calm,
Calm as the sea when the rude waves are laid,
And nothing but a gentle swell remains;
My curse is heard, and I shall have revenge:
There's something here which tells me 't will be so,
And peace resumes her empire o'er my breast.
Vardanes is the Minister of Vengeance;

Fir'd by ambition, he aspiring seeks
T' adorn his brows with *Parthia*'s diadem;
I've found the fire, and wrought him up to fury,
Envy shall urge him forward still to dare,
And discord be the prelude to destruction,
Then this detested race shall feel my hate.

#2—Dramatic
Evanthe: a young woman in love with Arsaces, the Prince of Parthia, 18–20

Evanthe was rescued from the evil Vonomes by his brother, the brave Arsaces. Here, she speaks of her love for the noble prince.

EVANTHE: No, I'll not meet him now, for love delights
in the soft pleasures of the secret shade,
And shuns the noise and tumult of the croud.
How tedious are the hours which bring him
To my fond panting heart! for oh! to those
Who live in expectation of the bliss,
Time slowly creeps, and ev'ry tardy minute
Seems mocking of their wishes. Say, *Cleone*,
For you beheld the triumph, midst his pomp,
Did he not seem to curse the empty show,
The pageant greatness, enemy to love,
Which held him from *Evanthe?* haste, to tell me,
And feed my greedy ear with the fond tale—
Yet, hold   for I shall weary you with questions,
And ne'er be satisfied— Beware, *Cleone*,
And guard your heart from Love's delusive sweets.
[*CLEONE:* Is Love an ill, that thus you caution me,
To shun his pow'r?]
EVANTHE: The Tyrant, my *Cleone*,
Despotic rules, and fetters all our thoughts.
Oh! wouldst thou love, then bid adieu to peace,
Then fears will come, and jealousies intrude,
Ravage your bosom, and disturb your quiet,
E'en pleasure to excess will be a pain.
Once I was free, then my exulting heart
Was like a bird that hops from spray to spray,

And all was innocence and mirth; but, lo!
The Fowler came, and by his arts decoy'd,
And soon the Wanton cag'd. Twice fifteen times
Has *Cynthia* dipt her horns in beams of light.
Twice fifteen times has wasted all her brightness,
Since first I knew to love; 't was on that day
When curs'd *Vonones* fell upon the plain,
The lovely Victor doubly conquer'd me.

The Provoked Wife

Sir John Vanbrugh
1697

Scene: England

Serio-Comic

Lady Brute: a woman unhappy with her husband, 20–30

Sir John has been treating her very poorly as of late and here the provoked woman takes a moment to blow off a little steam.

LADY BRUTE: The devil's in the fellow, I think. I was told before I married him that thus 'twould be. But I thought I had charms enough to govern him, and that where there was an estate, a woman must needs be happy. So my vanity has deceived me, and my ambition has made me uneasy. But some comfort still: if one would be revenged of him, these are good times. A woman may have a gallant and a separate maintenance[10] too. The surly puppy! Yet he's a fool for't. For hitherto he has been no monster;[11] but who knows how far he may provoke me? I never loved him, yet I have been ever true to him, and that in spite of all the attacks of art and nature upon a poor weak woman's heart in favour of a tempting lover. Methinks so noble a defence as I have made should be rewarded with a better usage. Or who can tell? Perhaps a good part of what I suffer from my husband may be a judgment upon me for my cruelty to my lover. Lord, with what pleasure could I indulge that thought were there but a possibility of finding arguments to make it good. And how do I know but there may? Let me see. What opposes? My matrimonial vow? Why, what did I vow? I think I promised to be true to my husband. Well, and he promised to be kind to me. But he han't kept his word. Why then I'm absolved from mine. Ay, that seems clear to me. The argument's good between the king and the people; why not between the husband and wife? Oh, but that condition was not expressed. No matter; 'twas understood. Well, by all I see, if I argue the matter a little longer with myself, I shan't find so many bugbears in the way as I thought I should. Lord, what fine no-

---

[10]Maintenance: an allowance from an estranged husband.
[11]Monster: cuckold.

tions of virtue do we women take up upon the credit of old foolish philosophers. Virtue's its own reward, virtue's this, virtue's that. Virtue's an ass, and a gallant's worth forty on't.

Psyche Debauched

Thomas Duffett
1678

Scene: mytho-poetic England

#1—Serio-Comic
    Ambition: presented as an Alderman's wife, any age.

Here, Ambition appears to a young country girl and offers to teach her the ways of the world.

AMBITION: I come to fetch you from this life of Beast,

To grand Solemnity of City Feast;

Leave smoaky Cot, and Cake-bread tough,

There's Custards hot, and Fools enough:

Leave Tib and Tom, for good House-holder,

There's Capon fat, and Mutton shoulder.

Leave Eldern whistle, Gut of Cats,

For City Horn-pipe and Waits;

By me ev'n Mrs. *Steward* you shall sit,

Whose Lilly hand carves every bit.

And tells the price to show housewifely Wit,

Lump shall be carri'd home too in Kerchief Wallet;

Or else it shall go hard in faith la, shall se't,

By me to noble thoughts you shall be brought,

And all the Arts of City Madam taught.

Locket on Arm, Ring on Finger,

Of Bobs too, in each ear a Clinger;

With fingers end, or Diamond Ring to play,

And cry, Oh Lord! when you have nought to say;

Finely to stretch, or show the pouting lip,

I'le teach you when to cry foro'th, or sip;

I'le teach you how to filtch and spend

Dull Husbands muck on courtly Friend;

Yet with grave mouth to rail at th'other end

Of this wild Town.—

Leave boars with limbs more stiff and hard then Oak,

And think of ruling sparks in Camlet Cloak;

Fresh Sweet-hearts every day new love shall swear:
And in all junckets, who but *None-so-fair*?
Come, come, wed rich retailing Prince; be Great,
Sit finely drest in Shop, serve God, and cheat.

#2—Serio-Comic
    Redstreak: the wife of a simple countryman, 30s

Here, this good-hearted provincial woman fantasizes about what it would be like to
be Queen.

REDSTREAK: Now for me, I'le be a Queen or a Lady at least; and King
Andrew's Three Daughters shall be my Maids, and I'le have a high Seat
in the Church, and the Chaplain shall pray for his virtuous Patrons.—
Then I'le have the head-ach, and be very sick, that I may receive Visits
in my Bed, Oh! there's no way like it to draw on Sutors; they know a
poor weak Woman that lyes there on purpose, has no power to deny.—
One that I know, drest her self in six several dresses to catch her Sweetheart, but nothing pleas'd her, I'le warrant you, 'till she fucust her face,
blanch'd her hands, put on a rich suit of Night Linnen, and went to
Bed; where she lay like a Queen Apple upon a Tod of Wool, and the
Patches look'd for all the World like Birds pecks, which show the Fruit
is Rotten-ripe; and what do'e think? the Whore-Son snuffed up his
Nose, and cry'd he did not love brown crust in Milk; a proud Jack. I'le
make a Law that every man shall be hang'd that refuseth a Woman; ay
and 'tis high time, for we have been even so kind to'm, that they use us
as they do Rackets at Tennis, when they have exercised their Bodies
and thump'd their Balls,—dress, and away; but my Lady *Redstreak*,
won't be served so ifaith.—After Dinner the Steward shall set things
right with me in my Closet, and the Gentleman of the Horse, or some
spruce fellow shall Fiddle me asleep. Oh *Redstreak*, didst thou ever
think to come to this? But if this should be a lye, now I am bravely
served.—

The Relapse or Virtue in Danger

Sir John Vanbrugh

1696

Scene: England

Dramatic

Amanda: an unhappy wife, 20–30

Amanda has just discovered her wayward husband in the arms of another woman. Here, she fumes as she contemplates her response.

AMANDA: (*Alone*.) At last I am convinc'd. My eyes are testimonies of his falsehood.

The base, ungrateful, perjur'd villain—

Good gods—what slippery stuff are men compos'd of?

Sure the account of their creation's false,

And 'twas the woman's rib that they were form'd of.

But why am I thus angry?

This poor relapse should only move my scorn.

'Tis true, the roving flights of his unfinish'd youth

Had strong excuse from the plea of Nature:

Reason had thrown the reins loose on his neck,

And slipt him to unlimited desire

If therefore he went wrong, he had a claim

To my forgiveness, and I did him right.

But since the years of manhood rein him in,

And reason, well digested into thought,

Has pointed out the course he ought to run;

If now he strays?

'Twould be as weak and mean in me to pardon,

As it has been in him t'offend. But hold:

'Tis an ill cause indeed, where nothing's to be said for't.

My beauty possibly is in the wane:

Perhaps sixteen has greater charms for him:

Yes, there's the secret. But let him know,

My quiver's not entirely empty'd yet,

I still have the darts, and I can shoot 'em too;

They're not so blunt, but they can enter still;

The want's not in my power, but in my will.
Virtue's his friend; or, through another's heart,
I yet could find the way to make his smart.

The Rival Queens or The Death of Alexander the Great

Nathaniel Lee
1690

Scene: Babylon

#1—Dramatic
> Statira: wife of Alexander the Great, a woman possessed by great passion and jealousy, 20–30

> Those who conspire against Alexander have told Statira that her husband has broken his vow to her by sleeping with Roxana, his second wife. Here, the Queen reacts with jealous grief.

STATIRA: Give me a knife, a draught of poison, flames;
Swell, heart; break, break, thou stubborn thing.
Now, by the sacred fire, I'll not be held;
Why do you wish me life, yet stifle me
For want of air? Pray give me leave to walk.
[SYSIGAMBIS: Is there no reverence to my person due?
Darius would have heard me. Trust not rumor.]
STATIRA: No, he hates,
He loathes the beauties which he has enjoyed.
O, he is false, that great, that glorious man
Is tyrant midst of his triumphant spoils,
Is bravely false to all the gods, forsworn.
Yet who would think it? No, it cannot be,
It cannot. What, that dear, protesting man!
He that has warmed my feet with thousand sighs,
Then cooled 'em with his tears, died on my knees,
Outwept the morning with his dewy eyes,
And groaned and swore the wond'ring stars away?
[SYSIGAMBIS: No, 'tis impossible; believe thy mother
That knows him well.]
STATIRA: Away, and let me die.
O, 'tis my fondness, and my easy nature
That would excuse him; but I know he's false,
'Tis now the common talk, the news o'th' world,
False to Statira, false to her that loved him.

That loved him, cruel Victor as he was,
And took him bathed all 'o'er in Persian blood,
Kissed the dear, cruel wounds, and washed 'em o'er
And o'er in tears; then bound 'em with my hair,
Laid him all night upon my panting bosom,
Lulled like a child, and hushed him with my songs.
[*PARISATIS:* If this be true, ah, who will ever trust
A man again?]
STATIRA: A man! A man! My Parisatis,
Thus with thy hand held up, thus let me swear thee.
By the eternal body of the sun,
Whose body, O, forgive the blasphemy,
I loved not half so well as the least part
Of my dear, precious, faithless Alexander;
For I will tell thee, and to warn thee of him,
Not the spring's mouth, nor breath of jessamine,
Nor violets' infant sweets, nor opening buds
Are half so sweet as Alexander's breast;
From every pore of him a perfume falls,
He kisses softer than a southern wind,
Curls like a vine, and touches like a god.
[*SYSIGAMBIS:* When will thy spirits rest, these transports cease?]
STATIRA: Will you not give me leave to warn my sister?
As I was saying—but I told his sweetness.
Then he will talk, good gods, how he will talk!
Even when the joy he sighed for is possessed,
He speaks the kindest words and looks such things,
Vows with such passion, swears with so much grace,
That 'tis a kind of heaven to be deluded by him.
[*PARISATIS:* But what was it that you would have me swear?]
STATIRA: Alas, I had forget. Let me walk by
And weep awhile, and I shall soon remember.

Following an emotional reconciliation with Alexander, Statira awaits him in her bed chamber. While she dozes, the ghosts of her parents appear in a dream to warn her of her impending death. When she wakens, she contemplates his unhappy visitation.

STATIRA: Bless me, ye pow'rs above, and guard my virtue!
I saw, nor was't a dream, I saw and heard
My royal parents; there I saw 'em stand.
My eyes beheld their precious images;
I heard their heav'nly voices. Where, O, where
Fled you so fast, dear shades, from my embraces.
You told me this: this hour should be my last,
And I must bleed.—Away, 'tis all delusion!
Do not I wait for Alexander's coming?
None but my loving lord can enter here;
And will he kill me? Hence, fantastic shadows!
And yet methinks he should not stay thus long.
Why do I tremble thus? If I but stir,
The motion of my robes makes my heart leap
When will the dear man come, that all my doubts
May vanish in his breast? that I may hold him
Fast as my fears can make me, hug him close
As my fond soul can wish, give all my breath
In sighs and kisses, swoon, die away with rapture!
But hark, I hear him— (*Noise within.*)
Fain I would hide my blushes,
I hear his tread, but dare not go to meet him.

The Rivals

Richard Brinsley Sheridan
1775

Scene: Bath

Serio-Comic
Mrs. Malaprop: an opinionated dowager, 50s

Mrs. Malaprop's niece, Lydia, has refused to marry the well-appointed son of Sir Anthony Adverse. Sir Anthony blames the young lady's willfulness on her education, which he feels no young lady should have. Here, Mrs. Malaprop defends her decision to educate young women.

MRS. MALAPROP: Fie, fie, Sir Anthony, you surely speak laconically! [*SIR ANTHONY:* Why, Mrs. Malaprop, in moderation, now, what would you have a woman know?]
MRS. MALAPROP: Observe me, Sir Anthony. I would by no means wish a daughter of mine to be a progeny of learning; I don't think so much learning becomes a young woman; for instance—I would never let her meddle with Greek, or Hebrew, or Algebra, or Simony, or Fluxions, or Paradoxes, or such inflammatory branches of learning—neither would it be necessary for her to handle any of your mathematical, astronomical, diabolical instruments;—but, Sir Anthony, I would send her, at nine years old, to a boarding-school, in order to learn a little ingenuity and artifice. Then, Sir, she should have a supercilious knowledge in accounts—and as she grew up, I would have her instructed in geometry, that she might know something of the contagious countries—but above all, Sir Anthony, she should be mistress of orthodoxy, that she might not misspell, and mispronounce words so shamefully as girls usually do; and likewise that she might reprehend the true meaning of what she is saying. This, Sir Anthony, is what I would have a woman know—and I don't think there is superstitious article in it.

The Royal Mischief

Mary Delarivier Manley
1696

Scene: the middle east

Dramatic

> Bassima: a captured princess, 18–20

> Bassima has been married to the Prince of Colchis for political reasons. The unfortunate young woman soon finds herself pursued by Osman, the Prince's Grand Visier. Here, she does her best to dissuade the relentless Osman.

BASSIMA: 'Tis I then that should seek that land of ease,
For I am all which you have named,
Wretched, forlorn, and desperate. Oh, thou
Eternal power that first made fate,
If I have sinned, 'twas by your own decree.
Why send you passion of desire and joy,
And then command us those passions to destroy,
When long foreseeing that we can't do so,
Dooms us rewards of everlasting woe?
Where's then the kindness to their likeness shown,
Cast in a form they vainly call their own?
Fond ignorance, for they are all divine,
Exempt from what unhappy mortals fear,
Nor can their beings fail, like those who wander here.
Hence, then, thou false received belief, be gone,
And let us see we're like ourselves alone.
[*OSMAN:* Who gives my princess grief?]
BASSIMA: You, only you.
The Earth's united hatred could not harm
Me equal to your kindness. It strikes at
Innocence and fame, and lays my virtue
Level with the vilest,
Makes marriage and uneasy bondage,
And the embraces of my lord a loathsome
Penance. What would you more? The time is come
That I must speak to make my ruin certain.

Like some prophetic priestess, full of the
God that rends her, must breathe the baleful
Oracle or burst. My crowding stars just
Now appear to fight, and dart upon me
With malignant influence. Nor can my
Reason stop the dictates of my heart,
They echo from my mouth in sounds of love,
But such a love as never woman knew.
'Twas surely given by fate, I would have said
From Heaven, but that inspires but good,
And this is surely none.

The Tragedy of Jane Shore

Nicholas Rowe
1714

Scene: London, June 1483

#1—Dramatic
> Jane Shore: a woman fallen on hard times, 30s

Following the death of Edward IV, his brother, the Duke of Glouster, hastens to seize power. Jane Shore, a married woman of renowned beauty, was once the favorite of Edward, but now lives in poverty, her properties seized by Glouster. When her friend, Alicia, suggests that Jane learn to seek pity from the men who control her life, Jane makes the following reply.

JANE SHORE: Why should I think that man will do for me
What yet he never did for wretches like me?
Mark by what partial justice we are judged;
Such is the fate unhappy women find,
And such the curse entailed upon our kind,
That man, the lawless libertine, may rove
Free and unquestioned through the wilds of love;
While woman, sense and nature's easy fool,
If poor, weak woman swerve from virtue's rule,
If, strongly charmed, she leaves the thorny way,
And in the softer paths of pleasure stray;
Ruin ensues, reproach and endless shame,
And one false step entirely damns her fame,
In vain with tears the loss she may deplore,
In vain look back to what she was before;
She sets, like stars that fall, to rise no more.

#2—Dramatic
> Jane Shore

Alicia's treachery has caused Jane to be turned out of her home. Here, poor Jane wanders the streets, desperate and starving, and suddenly finds herself at Alicia's door.

JANE SHORE: (*Her hair hanging loose on her shoulders, and barefooted.*)
Yet, yet endure, nor murmur, O my soul!
For are not thy transgressions great and numberless?

Do they not cover thee, like rising floods,
And press thee like a weight of waters down?
Does not the hand of righteousness afflict thee;
And who shall plead against it? Who shall say
To pow'r almighty, 'Thou hast done enough:'
Or bid his dreadful rod of vengeance stay?
Wait then with patience till the circling hours
Shall bring the time of thy appointed rest
And lay thee down in death. The hireling thus
With labor drudges out the painful day,
And often looks with long expecting eyes
To see the shadows rise and be dismissed.
And hark! methinks the roar that late pursued me
Sinks like the murmurs of a falling wind,
And softens into silence. Does revenge
And malice then grow weary, and forsake me?
My guard, too, that observed me still so close,
Tire in the task of their inhuman office
And loiter far behind. Alas, I faint;
My spirits fail at once. This is the door
Of my Alicia—blessèd opportunity!
I'll steal a little succor from her goodness
Now, while no eye observes me.
(*She knocks at the door.*)

The Tragedy of Zara

Aaron Hill, Esq.

@1750

Scene: Jerusalem

Dramatic

Zara: a slave in love with the Sultan of Jerusalem, 18–20

Zara was brought to Jerusalem as a child and though a Christian, raised Saracen. She has grown up to be the favorite of the Sultan, who plans to marry her as soon as possible. When Selima, another slave, asks Zara how it is possible for her to turn her back on her Christian heritage, she makes the following reply.

ZARA: Can my fond heart, on such a feeble proof,
Embrace a faith, abhorr'd by him I love?
I see too plainly custom forms us all;
Our thoughts, our morals, our most fix'd belief,
Are consequences of our place of birth:
Born beyond the Ganges I had been a Pagan,
In France a Christian, I am here a Saracen:
'Tis but instruction, all! Our parents' hand
Writes on our heart the first faint characters,
Which time, re-tracing, deepens into strength,
That nothing can efface, but death or Heaven!—
Thou wer t not made a pris'ner in this place,
'Till after reason, borrowing force from years,
Had lent its lustre to enlighten faith:—
For me, who in my cradle was their slave,
Thy Christian doctrines were too lately taught me:
Yet, far from having lost the rev'rence due,
This cross, as often as it meets my eye,
Strikes thro' my heart a kind of awful fear!
I honour, from my soul, the Christian laws,
Those laws, which, softening nature by humanity,
Melt nations into brotherhood;—no doubt,
Christians are happy; and 'tis just to love them.

Venice Preserved or
A Plot Discovered

Thomas Otway
1682

Scene: Venice

Dramatic
      Belvidera: a young woman trapped in an unhappy marriage, 18–20

Belvidera's husband, Jaffeir, has just joined in a conspiracy against the Venetian Senate, of which her father is a member. When she forces Jaffier to turn in his fellow
conspirators, the guilt he feel at his betrayal eventually drives him to an attempt on
Belvidera's life. Here, she confronts her father and begs him to release Jaffier's
friends from prison.

BELVIDIRA: Oh, my husband, my dear husband
Carries a dagger in his once kind bosom
To pierce the heart of your poor Belvidera.
[*PRIU:* Kill Thee!]
BELVIDIRA: Yes, kill me. When he pass'd his faith
And covenant against your state and Senate,
He gave me up as hostage for his truth,
With me a dagger and a dire commission,
Whene'er he fail'd, to plunge it through his bosom.
I learnt the danger, chose the hour of love
T'attempt his heart, and bring it back to honour.
Great love prevail'd and bless'd me with success.
He came, confess'd, betray'd his dearest friends
For promis'd mercy; now they're doom'd to suffer.
Gall'd with remembrance of what then was sworn,
If they are lost, he vows t'appease the gods
With this poor life, and make my blood th'atonement.
[*PRIU:* Heavens!]
BELVIDIRA: Think you saw what pass'd at our last parting,
Think you beheld him like a raging lion,
Pacing the earth and tearing up his steps,
Fate in his eyes, and roaring with the pain
Of burning fury; think you saw his one hand

Fix'd on my throat, while the extended other
Grasp'd a keen, threat'ning dagger. Oh, 'twas thus
We last embrac'd; when, trembling with revenge,
He dragg'd me to the ground, and at my bosom
Presented horrid death, cried out, "My friends,
Where are my friends?" swore, wept, rag'd, threaten'd, lov'd,
For he yet lov'd, and that dear love preserv'd me
To this last trial of a father's pity.
I fear not death, but cannot bear a thought
That that dear hand should do th' unfriendly office;
If I was ever then your care, now hear me;
Fly to the Senate, save the promis'd lives
Of his dear friends, ere mine be made the sacrifice.
[PRIU: Oh, my heart's comfort!]
BELVIDIRA: Will you not, my father?
Weep not, but answer me.

The Way to Keep Him

Arthur Murphy
1760

Scene: London

Serio-Comic
> Muslin: a saucy lady's maid, 20–30

> When her mistress complains about not being able to keep her husband interested in their marriage, the knowing young maid offers both chastisement and advice.

MUSLIN: No comfort, Ma'am? Whose fault then? Would anybody but you, Ma'am? It provokes me to think of it. Would anybody, Ma'am, young and handsome as you are, with so many accomplishments, Ma'am, sit at home here, as melancholy as a poor servant out of place? And all this for what? Why for a husband, and such a husband! What do you think the world will say of you, Ma'am, if you go on this way? [*MRS. LOVEMORE:* I care not what they say, I am tired of the world, and the world may be tired of me, if it will: my troubles are my own only, and I must endeavour to bear them.—Who knows what patience may do? If Mr. Lovemore has any feeling left, my resignation may some day or other have its effect, and incline him to do me justice.] *MUSLIN:* But, dear Ma'am, that's waiting for dead men's shoes—incline him to do you justice! What signifies expecting and expecting? Give me a bird in the hand.—Lard, Ma'am, to be for ever pining and grieving! Dear heart! If all the women in London, in your case, were to sit down and die of the spleen, what would become of all the public places? They might turn Vauxhall to a hop-garden, make a brewhouse of Ranelagh, and let both the playhouses to a Methodist preacher. We should not have the racketting[12] with 'em we have now.—'John, let the horses be put to.'—'John, go to my Lady Trumpabout's, and invite her to a small party of twenty or thirty card tables.'—'John, run to my Lady Cat-Gut, and let her Ladyship know I'll wait on her to the new opera.'—'John, run as fast as ever you can, with my compliments to Mr. Varney,[13] and tell him I shall take it as the greatest favour on earth, if he will let me have a side-box for the new play.—No excuse, tell

[12]Living a gay, social life; "gadding about."
[13]In charge of advance bookings at Drury Lane.

him.'—They whisk about the town, and rantipole[14] it with as unconcerned looks, and as florid outsides, as if they were treated at home like
so many goddesses, though everybody knows possession has ungod-
dessed them all long ago, and their husbands care no more for them—
no, by jingo, nor more than they do for their husbands.

[*MRS. LOVEMORE:* You run on at a strange rate.]

MUSLIN: (*In a passion.*) Dear Ma'am, 'tis enough to make a body run
on.—If everybody thought like you—

[*MRS. LOVEMORE:* If everybody loved like me—]

MUSLIN: A brass thimble for love, if it is not answered by love.—What
the deuce is here to do? Shall I go and fix my heart upon a man, that
shall despise me for that very reason, and, 'Ay,' says he, 'poor fool, I
see she loves me—the woman's well enough, only she has one inconve-
nient circumstance about her: I'm married to her, and marriage is the
Devil.'—And then when he's going a-roguing, smiles impudently in
your face, and, 'My dear, divert yourself, I'm just going to kill half an
hour at the chocolate-house, or to peep in at the play; your servant, my
dear, your servant.'—Fie upon 'em! I know 'em all.—Give me a husband that will enlarge the circle of my innocent pleasures: but a husband nowadays, Ma'am, is no such a thing.—A husband now, as I hope
for mercy, is nothing at all but a scarecrow, to show you the fruit, but
touch it if you dare.—A husband—the Devil take 'em all—Lord forgive
one for swearing—is nothing at all but a bugbear, a snapdragon; a husband, Ma'am, is—

[*MRS. LOVEMORE:* Prithee, peace with your tongue, and see what
keeps that girl.]

MUSLIN: Yes, Ma'am.—Why, Jenny, why don't you come up to my
mistress? What do you stand a-gossiping there for? A husband, Ma'am,
is a mere monster; that is to say, if one makes him so; then, for certain,
he is a monster indeed; and if one does not make him so, then he be-
haves like a monster; and of the two evils, by my troth—Ma'am, was
you ever at the play of Catherine and Mercutio?[15] The vile man calls his
wife his goods, and his cattles, and his household stuff.—There you
may see, Ma'am, what a husband is—a husband is—but here comes

---

[14]Behave in a noisy fashion.
[15]She means "Petruchio." *Catherine and Petruchio* was Garrick's 1756 alteration of *The Tam-
ing of the Shrew.*

one will tell you—here comes Sir Brilliant Fashion.—Ask his advice, Ma'am.

[*MRS. LOVEMORE:* His advice! Ask advice of the man who has estranged Mr. Lovemore's affections from me!]

MUSLIN: Well, I protest and vow, Ma'am, I think Sir Brilliant a very pretty gentleman.—He's the very pink of the fashion; he dresses fashionably, lives fashionably, wins your money fashionably, loses his own fashionably, and does everything fashionably; and then, he is so lively, and talks so lively, and so much to say, and so never at a loss.—But here he comes.

The Wife of Bath

John Gay

1713

Scene: an inn lying on the road between London and Canterbury

Serio-Comic

Alison: the wife of Bath, 20–30

When a fellow traveler claims to have been visited by an apparition, this earthy woman reveals her knowledge of the spirit world.

ALISON: The very downright Symptoms of a Spirit!—a Spirit as certainly attacks your Nostrils with the Fumes of Sulphur, as a Beau with a Digestion of a Civet.—I think I do smell it,—Yes, yes, I do smell it. [*MYRTILLA:* You seem to be frighten'd.]

ALISON: Frighten'd! quotha—No, no, Madam,—I have, thanks to Experience, seen Spirits of all Shapes, and all Countries—Why, a *Jerusalem* Spirit is no more like an *English* Spirit than a Hog is like a Rhinoceros — I have been Witness of all the Devil's Frolicks—Idad, to my certain Knowledge, he makes nothing of unfurnishing a Kitchen to entertain himself with a Country-Dance of Dishes and Platters; many be the times and often, he has rattled my Curtains, and made the Bed shake under me, when I have not had the comfort of a Bedfellow; many a dark Night have I seen the Headless Horse, and have had the Honour to Converse with the Queen of the Fairies. (*Looking towards the Table.*) Hah, hah, Damsel! Cake and a Bottle!—Heighday!—and St. *Agnes*'s Night too!—are you thereabouts, Girl—'Twas a Ghost I perceive of your own raising, my Dear, ha, ha, ha.

[*MYRTILLA:* Your contradicting my former Fortune, Madam, drew me in to commit this new piece of Folly.]

ALISON: Come, Honey,—here is his Health,—with all my Heart. (*Sings.*)

The Maiden and the Batchelor,
  Pardie— are simple Elves,
And 'till they grow to Man and Wife,
  Know nothing of themselves.

Then since we're each others by Nature design'd

Let's unite, and our Knowledge improve;
Here's a Health to the Lass that is passively kind,
    And the Youth that is active in Love. (Drinks.)

—S'heartlikins, Madam, the very Expectation has embellished your Phisiognomy; then what may we not hope from the Possession?—Tell me now, Honey, did not his Appearance make the Blood shoot through your Veins, and tickle your Heart's Root?

Men's Monologues

All for Love or
The World Well Lost

John Dryden
1678

Scene: Alexandria

#1—Dramatic
Mark Antony: General of Rome, 40s

On the last day of his life, Mark Antony enjoys a dark and melancholy fantasy of his death.

ANTONY: (*Having thrown himself down.*)
Lie there, thou shadow of an emperor;
The place thou pressest on thy mother earth
Is all thy empire now: now it contains thee;
Some few days hence, and then 'twill be too large,
When thou'rt contracted in thy narrow urn,
Shrunk to a few cold ashes; then Octavia
(For Cleopatra will not live to see it),
Octavia then will have thee all her own,
And bear thee in her widowed hand to Cæsar;
Cæsar will weep, the crocodile will weep,
To see his rival of the universe
Lie still and peaceful there. I'll think no more on't.
Give me some music; look that it be sad:
I'll soothe my melancholy, till I swell,
And burst myself with sighing.— (*Soft music.*)
'Tis somewhat to my humor. Stay, I fancy
I'm now turned wild, a commoner of nature,
Of all forsaken, and forsaking all;
Live in a shady forest's sylvan scene;
Stretched at my length beneath some blasted oak,
I lean my head upon the mossy bark,
And look just of a piece as I grew from it:
My uncombed locks, matted like mistletoe,
Hang o'er my hoary face; a murm'ring brook

Runs at my foot.

[*VENTIDIUS:* Methinks I fancy

Myself there too.]

ANTONY: The herd comes jumping by me,

And, fearless, quench their thirst, while I look on,

And take me for their fellow-citizen.

More of this image, more; it lulls my thoughts. (*Soft music again.*)

#2–Dramatic

Ventidius: faithful friend of Mark Antony and General of Rome, 40-50

When Ventidius discovers his old friend in Alexandria, he knows instinctively that Mark Antony's life has come to an end.

VENTIDIUS: Does the mute sacrifice upbraid the priest?

He knows him not his executioner.

Oh, she has deck'd his ruin with her love,

Led him in golden bands to gaudy slaughter,

And made perdition pleasing. She has left him

The blank of what he was.

I tell thee, eunuch, she has quite unmann'd him.

Can any Roman see and know him now,

Thus alter'd from the lord of half mankind,

Unbent, unsinew'd, made a woman's toy,

Shrunk from the vast extent of all his honours,

And cramp'd within a corner of the world?

O Antony,

Thou bravest soldier, and thou best of friends!

Bounteous as nature, next to nature's God!

Couldst thou but make new worlds, so wouldst thou give 'em,

As bounty were thy being. Rough in battle,

As the first Romans when they went to war;

Yet after victory more pitiful

Than all their praying virgins left at home!

Andromache

Jean Racine
1667

Scene: Epirus, after the fall of Troy

#1—Dramatic
> Orestes: the Greek Ambassador, 30–40

> Orestes has traveled to Epirus to pursue his love for Hermione, the daughter of Helen, and to take Hector's son prisoner. Here, he speaks of his unrequited love and his mission.

ORESTES: Alas, who knows what fate is guiding me?
Love sends me here, to seek a cruel mistress,
But I can never know what Fate has ordered,
Whether I come to find my life—or death.
[*PYLADES:* Then is your soul so bound in slavery
That you would live because of love, alone?
What spell has sent you to those flames again?
Forgetting all the tortures you have suffered?
Will she, who would not hear you pray in Sparta
Prove kinder, now she finds you in Epirus?
You should despise her; you should blush with shame
For vows so futile. Speak no more of her,
Your words deceived me.]
ORESTES: I deceived myself.
Oh, do not crush a wretch who loves you well.
What yearning have I ever hidden from you?
You knew my flame new-born, and my first sigh.
You saw how I despaired, when Menelaus
Made promise of his daughter's hand to Pyrrhus,—
He who avenged his race; and you have seen
How I dragged my chains from sea to sea.
I saw you, full of pity for my state
Ready to follow where I chanced to go.
Day after day you saved me from myself,
And checked my madness in its wild career.
But when I was distracted, when I thought

Of how Hermione was lavishing
Her charms on Pyrrhus, well you know I tried.
Filled with my anger, to repay her scorn
With my forgetfulness. Then you believed
And I, myself, believed the fight was won.
I thought my passion had been turned to hatred,
I mocked her charms, and thought that I abhorred her,
I loathed her coldness, I defied her eyes
To bring again the love I had crushed.
It was in that false calm I came to Greece,
And found the kings in arms against a danger,—
No little peril,—which had newly risen,
Heavy with troubles. Then, most eagerly
I joined them, for, indeed, I hoped to find
Freedom from other cares, in this new work,
I hoped that, if my strength came back to me
My heart would lose remembrance of its love.
But look you how my persecuting fates
Snared me the sooner in the trap I shunned.
I heard the threats and murmurs everywhere
Raised against Pyrrhus by the whole of Greece,
Which cried that Pyrrhus had forgot his promise
And his own blood, that at his court he harbors
The enemy of Greece, Astyanax,
The young and most unhappy son of Hector,
The child of many buried kings who lie
Beneath the walls of Troy. As I have heard,
Andromache deceived the great Ulysses
To save her baby,—for another child
Torn from her arms, was killed in place of him.
They tell me that Hermione has failed.
She has not won my rival; he has offered
To give his heart and kingdom to another.
Though Menelaus will not trust the rumor,
The long delay has tried his patience sorely,
To me, the very reason for his anger
Is my own secret triumph, though at first

I thought it but a fleeting revenge
A flattery of pride. But soon enough
I found my lovely persecutor taking
Her old place in my heart; the old fire burned,
I felt my hatred melt and quickly vanish,—
Or rather, knew I'd never ceased to love her.
I begged the aid of all the Greeks; they sent me
Here, where I am, to Pyrrhus, and the mission
Which brings me here is but to seize this child.
Many there are to fear him while he lives,
I come to snatch him out of Pyrrhus' arms,
Yet I should be most happy, could I capture
Not Hector's son indeed, but my own princess.
No, do not think this flame, which has been fanned
By being smothered long, can be extinguished
By any sort of peril. I've resisted
And proved resistance vain, and so I yield me
Blindly to passion; loving Hermione,
I come to win her, fly with her, or die.
You know this Pyrrhus. What will Pyrrhus do?
Tell me what happens in his court, and what
Passes within his heart. Is he still bound
To my Hermione; will he restore her,
And give me back the treasure he has stolen?

#2–Dramatic
Pyrrhus: son of Achilles, King of Epirus, 20–30

Pyrrhus has fallen in love with Andromache, the captive widow of Hector. Here, he offers to save her son from the Greeks if she will consent to marry him.

PYRRHUS: A moment, madam.
Your tears may still win back your son for you.
Yes; I regret that I have made you weep,
And gave you, thus, a sword to turn on me.
I thought I could have brought more hatred here,
At least you could consent to look at me!
Are these the eyes of justice, in its anger,
Taking its pleasure in your misery?

Why will you make me faithless to yourself?
Think of your son, and let us cease to hate.
Now it is I who urge it; save your son!
Must my own sighs beg that you spare his life?
And must I clasp your knees to plead for him?
Only this once! Save him and save yourself!
I know what solemn vows I break for you,
And how much hate I bring upon myself.
Hermione shall go, and on her brow
For crown, I'll set a burning brand of shame.
And in the temple, ready for her marriage
Andromache shall wear the diadem.
Lady, I offer this, and you will dare
No longer to disdain it. Rule or die!
A year of scorn has made me desperate,
And I am done with living still in doubt,
Torn by my fears, now making threats, now groaning.
I lose you, and I die,—and waiting longer
Is also death. I leave you to consider,
And soon I'll come to bring you to the temple,
And there my fury shall destroy this child,
Or else, in love, I'll crown you as my queen!

The Apprentice

Arthur Murphy, Esq.
@1809

Scene: an English Village

Serio-Comic

Dick: a young man with a flair for the dramatic, 18–20

Dick is a rascally youth who harbors a desire to make a life for himself on the stage. When he discovers it is his father's wish that he become an apprentice to an apothecary, he rejects the notion in the following melodramatic explosion.

DICK:[1](*Alone.*) Thus far we run before the wind.—An apothecary!— Make an apothecary of me!—[2] what, cramp my genius over a pestle and mortar, or mew up in a shop with an alligator stuffed, and a beggarly account of empty boxes!—to be culling simples, and constantly adding to the bills of mortality.—No! no! it will be much better to be pasted up in capitals, the part of Romeo by a young gentleman, who never appeared on any stage before!—my ambition fires at the thought—but hold,—mayn't I run some chance of failing in my attempt —hissed,—pelted,—laughed at,—not admitted into the green-room — that will never do—[3] down, busy devil, down, down.—Try it again.— Loved by the women, envied by the men, applauded by the pit, clapped by the gallery; admired by the boxes. "Dear colonel, is not he a charming creature?"—"my lord, don't you like him of all things?"— "makes love like an angel!"—"what an eye he has!—fine legs!" "I'll certainly go to his benefit."—Celestial sounds!—and then I'll get in with all the painters, and have myself put up in every print-shop—in the character of Macbeth! "this is a sorry sight." (*Stands in an attitude.*) In the character of Richard—"give me another horse, bind up my wounds."—This will do rarely—and then I have a chance of getting well married—O glorious thought!—[4] By heaven, I will enjoy it, though but in fancy—but what's o'clock?—it must be almost nine. I'll go away at once; this is a club-night.—'Egad I'll go to 'em for a while—the spouters are all met—little they think I'm in town—they'll be surprised

[1]Richard III.
[2]Romeo and Juliet.
[3]Venice Preserved.
[4]Tamerlane.

to see me—off I go, and then for my assignation with my master Gargle's daughter—poor Charlotte! she's locked up, but I shall find means to settle matters for her escape—she's a pretty theatrical genius—if she flies to my arms like a hawk to its perch, it will be so rare an adventure, and so dramatic an incident!—[5] Limbs, do your office, and support me well;

Bear me but to her, then fail me if you can.

---

[5]The Orphan.

The Beggar's Opera
John Gay
1728

Scene: London

Serio-Comic
Macheath: a notorious highwayman, 30s

Here, the infamous Macheath greets the strumpets he has summoned to his lair for an evening's entertainment.

MACHEATH: Dear Mrs. Coaxer, you are welcome. You look charmingly today. I hope you don't want the repairs of quality, and lay on paint.—Dolly Trull! kiss me, you slut; are you as amorous as ever, hussy? You are always so taken up with stealing hearts, that you don't allow yourself time to steal anything else.—Ah, Dolly, thou wilt ever be a coquette.—Mrs. Vixen, I'm yours; I always loved a woman of wit and spirit; they make charming mistresses, but plaguy wives.—Betty Doxy! Come hither, hussy. Do you drink as hard as ever? You had better stick to good wholesome beer; for in troth, Betty, strong waters will in time ruin your constitution. You should leave those to your betters.—What! and my pretty Jenny Diver too! As prim and demure as ever! There is not any prude, though ever so high bred, hath a more sanctified look, with a more mischievous heart. Ah! thou art a dear artful hypocrite.—Mrs. Slammekin! as careless and genteel as ever! all you fine ladies, who know your own beauty, affect an undress.—But see, here's Suky Tawdry come to contradict what I was saying. Everything she gets one way, she lays out upon her back. Why, Suky, you must keep at least a dozen tally-men.—Molly Brazen! (*She kisses him.*) That's well done. I love a free-hearted wench. Thou hast a most agreeable assurance, girl, and art as willing as a turtle.—But hark! I hear music. The harper is at the door. "If music be the food of love, play on." Ere you seat yourselves, ladies, what think you of a dance!—Come in. (*Enter Harper.*) Play the French tune, that Mrs. Slammekin was so fond of.

Cato

Joseph Addison
1713

Scene: Utica

Dramatic

Cato: Roman statesman who defied Cæsar, 40s

Conservative Cato backed Pompey in his struggle against Cæsar and then accompanied the losing general into exile. When Cato is informed of the defeat of the Roman nobility by Cæsar's legions in North Africa, he contemplates taking his own life.

(*Cato sitting in a thoughtful posture: in his hand Plato's book on the immortality of the soul. A drawn sword on the table by him.*)

CATO: It must be so—Plato, thou reason'st well!—
Else whence this pleasing hope, this fond desire,
This longing after immortality?
Or whence this secret dread, and inward horror,
of falling into nought? Why shrinks the soul
Back on herself, and startles at destruction?
'Tis the divinity that stirs within us;
'Tis heav'n itself, that points out an hereafter,
and intimates eternity to man.
Eternity! thou pleasing, dreadful thought!
Through what variety of untried being,
Through what new scenes and changes must we pass!
The wide, th' unbounded prospect, lies before me;
But shadows, clouds, and darkness, rest upon it.
Here will I hold. If there's a pow'r above us,
(And that there is all Nature cries aloud
Through all her works) he must delight in virtue:
And that which he delights in must be happy.
But when! or where!—This world was made for Cæsar.
I'm weary of conjectures—This must end 'em.
(*Laying his hand on his sword.*)
Thus am I doubly arm'd: my death and life,
My bane and antidote, are both before me:
This in a moment brings me to an end;

But this informs me that I shall never die.
The soul, secur'd in her existence, smiles
At the drawn dagger, and defies its point.
The stars shall fade away, the sun himself
Grow dim with age, and nature sink in years;
But thou shalt flourish in immortal youth,
Unhurt amidst the war of elements,
The wrecks of matter, and the crush of worlds.
What means this heaviness that hangs upon me?
This lethargy that creeps through all my senses?
Nature, oppress'd and harass'd out with care,
Sinks down to rest. This once I'll favour her,
That my awaken'd soul may take her flight,
Renew'd in all her strength, and fresh with life,
An off'ring fit for heav'n. Let guilt or fear
Disturb man's rest: Cato knows neither of 'em,
Indiff'rent in his choice to sleep or die.

The Confederacy

Sir John Vanbrugh
1705

Scene: London

Serio-Comic
> Brass

>> Brass and Dick are a couple of nefarious ne'er do-wells who have scrambled from
>> one scheme to the next with Dick always coming out on top of things. Here, Brass fi-
>> nally objects to always playing second fiddle.

BRASS: In short, look smooth, and be a good Prince, I am your Valet,
'tis true: Your Footman sometimes, which I enrag'd at; but you have always had the ascendant, I confess; when we were School-fellows, you
made me carry your Books, make your Exercise, own your Rogueries,
and sometimes take a Whipping for you: When we were Fellow-Pren-
tices, tho' I was your Senior, you made me open the Shop, clean my
Master's shoes, cut last at Dinner, and eat all the Crust. In our sins too, I
must own you still kept me under; you soar'd up to Adultery with our
Mistress, while I was at humble Fornication with the Maid. Nay, in our
Punishments, you still made good your Post; for when once upon a
time I was sentenced but to be Whip'd, I cannot deny but you were
condemn'd to be Hang'd. So that in all times, I must confess, your Incli-
nations have been greater and nobler than mine. However, I cannot
consent that you shou'd at once fix Fortune for Life, and I dwell in my
Humilities for the rest of my Days.

The Country Wife
William Wycherley
1675

Scene: London

Serio-Comic
> Pinchwife: a hypocritical husband, 20–30

> When the philandering Pinchwife discovers that his wife has written a letter to a gentleman admirer, he flies into a rage and threatens to kill her.

PINCHWIFE: How' this? Nay, you shall not stir, madam. 'Dear, dear, dear Mr Horner'—very well—I have taught you to write letters to good purpose! But let us see't. 'First, I am to beg your pardon for my boldness in writing to you, which I'd have you to know I would not have done, had not you said first you loved me so extremely, which if you do, you will never suffer me to lie in the arms of another man whom I loathe, nauseate, and detest.'—Now you can write these filthy words. But what follows?—'Therefore, I hope you will speedily find some way to free me from this unfortunate match, which was never, I assure you, of my choice, but I'm afraid 'tis already too far gone; however, if you love me, as I do you, you will try what you can do; but you must help me away before tomorrow, or else, alas, I shall be forever out of your reach, for I can defer no longer our—our—' What is to follow 'our'?— Speak, what? Our journey into the country, I suppose! O woman, damned woman! And Love, damned Love, their old tempter! For this is one of his miracles; in a moment he can make those blind that could see, and those see that were blind, those dumb that could speak, and those prattle who were dumb before;[6] nay, what is more than all, make these dough-baked,[7] senseless, indocile animals, women, too hard for us, their politic[8] lords and rulers, in a moment. But make and end of your letter, and then I'll make an end of you thus, and all my plagues together. (*Draws his sword.*)

---

[6] Pinchwife has a faulty memory for the words of Isaiah, 35, 5–6.
[7] Inadequately cooked; or foolish.
[8] Natural.

The Cheats

John Wilson
1662

Scene: London

Serio-Comic
Mopus: an "astrological physician," 30–50

Here, a glorified fortune teller muses over a book on astrology and wonders how to best bilk people out of their money.

MOPUS: Saturn and Jupiter come to a trine in Taurus and Capricorn. Huh! We shall have strangers come to town, and their wives ne'er miss 'em in the country. Next month they all meet in the house of Mercury, he being lord thereof and significator of speech: it may intend advocates, cryers of courts, splitters of causes, oyster wives, and broommen—Hold!—Saturn—(nothing but this malevolent planet) in the sign of Virgo, in conjunction with Venus in her detriment. Beware, women, of green gowns; great men, of stone and cholic; and costermongers, of rotten pippins. Again, *pars torturæ*, coupled with the *Catabibason*—that is to say, the Dragon's Tail—huh, huh—children shall be subject to convulsion fits, young wenches to the falling evil, and old women to cough out their teeth.—(*He makes a pause.*)—But all this is no money. Many an honest man has but one house, and maintains his family very well; but, such an unlucky rogue, the whole twelve will hardly pay my rent. Now, a pox take these citizens, and then a man might get some money by 'um. They are so hidebound, there's no living by 'um; so clunchfisted, a man would swear the gout were got out of their feet into their hands; 'tis death to 'um to pluck 'um out of their pockets. I am sure my bills bid as high as the proudest—they cure all diseases, and resolve all astrological questions, and they'll hardly quit cost for pasting 'um up. Here dwells an astrological physician, reads one; And there let him till I trouble him, answers another. His Majesty's most excellent operator, says one; Yes, upon post, quoth another. And thus you see how an artist is valued. O ignorance! ignorance! well may'st thou be mother of devotion; but I am sure thou art the step-dame of art. If it were not for the good women, with their groats and their vinegar bottles, and now and then a young wench to enquire of her sweetheart, I might e'en hang myself; nay (which were worse), my wife would cry her trade were the better o' th' two. But husht! I hear somebody coming. Ten to one but 'tis my young Squire, with his mercer's wife to have her fortune read—I could with less trouble and more certainty have told her husband's. I hear 'um—husht!—my wife understood their meaning, and might have put 'um together without troubling of me.

Dione

John Gay
@1720

Scene: Arcadia

Dramatic

Lycidas: a young man hopelessly in love with a nymph, 20s

Lycidas has forsaken everything in order to pursue Parthenia, a lovely nymph who eludes his every advance. Here, the love struck young man has finally discovered Parthenia asleep in the woods, and marvels at her sleeping beauty.

LYCIDAS: May no rude wind the rustling branches move;
Breathe soft, ye silent gales, nor wake my Love.
Ye shepherds, piping homeward on the way,
Let not the distant ecchoes learn your lay;
Strain not, ye nightingales, your warbling throat,
May no loud shake prolong the shriller note,
Lest she awake; O sleep, secure her eyes,
That I may gaze; for if she wake, she flies.
While easy dreams compose her peaceful soul,
What anxious cares within my bosom roll!
If tir'd with sighs beneath the beech I lye,
And languid slumber close my weeping eye,
Her lovely vision rises to my view,
Swift flys the nymph, and swift would I pursue;
I strive to call, my tongue has lost its sound;
Like rooted oaks, my feet benumm'd are bound;
Struggling I wake. Again my sorrows flow,
And not one flatt'ring dream deludes my woe.
What innocence! how meek is ev'ry grace!
How sweet the smile that dimples on her face,
Calm as the sleeping seas! but should my sighs
Too rudely breathe, what angry storms would rise!
Though the fair rose with beauteous blush is crown'd,
Beneath her fragrant leaves the thorn is found;
The peach, that with inviting crimson blooms,
Deep at the heart the cank'ring worm consumes;
'Tis thus, alas! those lovely features hide

Disdain and anger and resentful pride.
Hath proffer'd greatness yet o'ercome her hate?
And does she languish for the glitt'ring bait?
Against the swain she might her pride support.
Can she subdue her sex, and scorn a Court?
Perhaps in dreams the shining vision charms,
And the rich bracelet sparkles on her arms;
In fancy'd heaps the golden treasure glows:
Parthenia, wake; all this thy swain bestows.

Douglas

John Home
1757

Scene: Lord Randolph's castle in the west of Scotland, 12th century

#1—Dramatic
Glenalvon: a villain of dark passion, 30s

A man driven by forbidden desire, Glenalvon here reveals his passion for Lady Randolph, the wife of his uncle and benefactor. Lady Randolph has recently taken in a young stranger, and Glenalvon believes that she loves the unknown young man. Here, Glenalvon vows to find the stranger and kill him.

GLENALVON: Child that I was, to start at my own shadow,
And be the shallow fool of coward conscience!
I am not what I have been: what I should be.
The darts of destiny have almost pierced
My marble heart. Had I one grain of faith
In holy legends, and religious tales,
I should conclude there was an arm above
That fought against me, and malignant turned;
To catch myself, the subtle snare I set.
Why, rape and murder are not simple means!
Th' imperfect rape to Randolph gave a spouse;
And the intended murder introduced
A favorite to hide the sun from me;
And, worst of all, a rival. Burning hell!
This were thy center, if I thought she loved him!
'Tis certain she contemns me; nay, commands me,
And waves the flag of her displeasure o'er me,
In his behalf. And shall I thus be braved?
Curbed, as she calls it, by dame chastity?
Infernal fiends, if any fiends there are
More fierce than hate, ambition, and revenge,
Rise up and fill my bosom with your fires,
And policy remorseless! Chance may spoil
A single aim; but perseverance must
Prosper at last. For chance and fate are words:
Persistive wisdom is the fate of man.

Darkly a project peers upon my mind,
Like the red moon when rising in the east,
Crossed and divided by strange-colored clouds.
I'll seek the slave who came with Norval hither,
And for his cowardice was spurned from him.
I've known a follower's rankled bosom breed
Venom most fatal to his heedless lord.

#2—Dramatic
Douglas: a young man who has just discovered his true identity, 18–20

Douglas believed he was the son of a simple shepherd until Lady Randolph informs him that he is, in fact, her long-lost son. Following a poignant meeting with the good-hearted man who raised him, Douglas rejoices at being reunited with his true mother.

DOUGLAS: He loves me like a parent;
And must not, shall not, lose the son he loves,
Although his son has found a nobler father.
Eventful day! how hast thou changed my state!
Once on the cold and winter shaded side
Of a bleak hill, mischance had rooted me,
Never to thrive, child of another soil:
Transplanted now to the gay sunny vale,
Like the green thorn of May my fortune flowers.
Ye glorious stars! high heav'n's resplendent host!
To whom I oft have of my lot complained,
Hear and record my soul's unaltered wish!
Dead or alive, let me but be renowned!
May heav'n inspire some fierce gigantic Dane,
To give a bold defiance to our host!
Before he speaks it out I will accept;
Like Douglas conquer, or like Douglas die.

The Fair Penitent

Nicholas Rowe
1703

Scene: Genoa

Dramatic

Horatio: a young gentleman caught in an unpleasant situation, 20s

Horatio is married to Lavinia, the sister of his best friend, Altamont. Here, he discovers a letter written by Altamont's fiancée, Calista to the notorious Lothario. It is obvious that although she has accepted Altamont, Calista still lusts after womanizing Lothario. When he has finished reading this most illicit love letter, poor Horatio wonders what he should do.

HORATIO: Sure, 'tis the very error of my eyes:
Walking, I dream, or I behold Lothario;
He seemed conferring with Calista's woman;
At my approach they started, and retired.
What business could he have here, and with her?
I know he bears the noble Altamont
Professed and deadly hate—What paper's this? (*Taking up the letter.*)
Ha! to Lothario.—
'Sdeath! Calista's name! (*Opening it.*)
Confusion and misfortune! (*Reads.*)
"Your cruelty has at length determined me, and I have resolved this morning to yield a perfect obedience to my father, and to give my hand to Altamont, in spite of my weakness for the false Lothario. I could almost wish I had that heart and that honor to bestow with it which you have robbed me of—"
Damnation!—to the rest— (*Reads again.*)
"But oh! I fear, could I retrieve 'em, I should again be undone by the too faithless, yet too lovely Lothario; this is the last weakness of my pen, and tomorrow shall be the last in which I will indulge my eyes. Lucilla shall conduct you, if you are kind enough to let me see you; it shall be the last trouble you shall meet with from
The lost Calista."
The lost, indeed! for thou art gone as far
As there can be perdition. Fire and sulphur,
Hell is the sole avenger of such crimes.

O that the ruin were but all thy own!
Thou wilt ev'n make thy father curse his age;
At sight of this black scroll the gentle Altamont
(For oh! I know his heart is set upon thee)
Shall droop and hang his discontented head
Like merit scorned by insolent authority,
And never grace the public with his virtues.—
Perhaps ev'n now he gazes fondly on her,
And thinking soul and body both alike,
Blesses the perfect workmanship of heaven;
Then sighing, to his ev'ry care speaks peace,
And bids his heart be satisfied with happiness.
O wretched husband! while she hangs about thee
With idle blandishment, and plays the fond one,
Ev'n then her hot imagination wanders,
Contriving riots and loose shapes of love;
And while she clasps thee close, makes thee a monster.
What if I give this paper to her father?
It follows that his justice dooms her dead,
And breaks my heart with sorrow; hard return
For all the good his hand has heaped on us.
Hold, let me take a moment's thought.

False Delicacy

Hugh Kelly
1767

Scene: London

Serio-Comic
    Cecil: a man with a secret love, 40–50

> After promising to help his nephew court a certain young lady, Cecil takes a moment to ponder the dramatic changes that love tends to make in our lives.

CECIL: For a torrent of rapture and nonsense! What egregious puppies does this unaccountable love make of young fellows: Nay, for that matter, what egregious puppies does it not make of old ones? *Ecce signum!*[9] 'Tis a comfort, though, that nobody knows I am a puppy in this respect but myself. Here was I, fancying that all the partiality I felt for poor Hortensia Marchmont proceeded from my friendship for her father; when, upon an honest examination into my own heart, I find it principally arises from my regard for herself. I was in hopes a change of objects would have driven the baggage out of my thoughts, and I went to France; but I am come home with a settled resolution of asking her to marry a slovenly rascal of fifty, who is, to be sure, a very likely swain for a young lady to fall in love with. But who knows! The most sensible women have sometimes strange tastes; and yet it must be a very strange taste that can possibly approve of my overtures. I'll go cautiously to work, however,—and solicit her as for a friend of my own age and fortune; so that if she refuses me, which is probable enough, I shan't expose myself to her contempt. What a ridiculous figure is an old fool sighing at the feet of a young woman! Zounds, I wonder how the grey-headed dotards have the impudence to ask a blooming girl of twenty to throw herself upon a moving mummy, or a walking skeleton.

---

[9]Behold an instance.

The False Servant

Marivaux

1724

Scene: a country estate in France

Serio-Comic

Trivelin: an adventurer returned home, 30–40

After making his way in the world for 15 years, this crafty opportunist has returned home. Here, he delivers a philosophical description of his life to an old friend.

TRIVELIN: Over the fifteen odd years that I've been making my way in this world of ours, you know the lengths to which I've gone in my attempt to settle down. It had come to my notice that scrupulous men rarely make money. So, to give myself an even chance, I laid scruple aside. If it was profitable to be honorable, then I was a man of honour. If I deemed it pertinent to be devious, then, once my conscience had heaved a deep sigh of regret, I was devious. On occasions I have indeed been rich. But how is one to lend permanence to such a situation, when our path is littered with rocks? The odd flutter, the odd fling, the odd beverage. How is one to avoid temptation?

[*FRONTIN:* True.]

TRIVELIN: What else can I say? One day upstairs. The next day downstairs. Ever prudent. Ever industrious. Befriending crooks by design and gentlemen by inclination. Respected in one disguise, horsewhipped in another. Swapping employment, clothes, lifestyle, personality. Taking risks. Making peanuts. On the surface respectable, deep down a libertine. Suspected by some, spotted by others, dubious for everyone. I owe money left, right, and centre. My debtors fall into two categories. Those who don't know they lent me money. And those who do. And who will continue to know that I do for a long time yet. My lodgings? Anywhere and everywhere. Pavement, inn, doss-house. I've been entertained by the bourgeois and the aristocrat. Even had my own place once. And, when I fell on hard times, the halls of justice extended their welcoming arms. But these latter apartments are somewhat gloomy. So I chose not to stay too long. In all, my dear friend, after fifteen years of blood, sweat and tears, this unprepossessing packet is all I own. This is what the world has chosen to give me. Pretty mean, don't you think? My contribution deserves a larger reward. Given so much. Received so little.

Fatal Curiosity

George Lillo
1737

Scene: Penryn in Cornwall

Dramatic
Old Wilmot: a man fallen on hard times, 50–60

Wilmot has lost both his fortune and his son, who has been missing at sea for seven years. Here, the beleaguered man muses on the nature of man's impermanence.

OLD WILMOT: (*Alone.*) The day is far advanced. The cheerful sun
Pursues with vigor his repeated course,
No labor less'ning, nor no time decaying
His strength, or splendor. Evermore the same,
From age to age his influence sustains
Dependent worlds, bestow both life and motion
On the dull mass that forms their dusky orbs,
Cheers them with heat, and gilds them with his brightness.
Yet man, of jarring elements composed,
Who posts from change to change, from the first hour
Of his frail being till his dissolution,
Enjoys the sad prerogative above him:
To think, and to be wretched. What is life
To him that's born to die? Or what that wisdom
Whose perfection ends in knowing we know nothing?
Mere contradictions all! A tragic farce,
Tedious though short, and without art elab'rate,
Ridiculously sad—

The Fatal Friendship

Catherine Trotter
1698

Scene: England

Dramatic

Gramont: a young man in big trouble, 20s

Gramont's secret marriage to Felicia has brought both of them nothing but misery. Gramont's father has also fallen in love with Felicia, and—not knowing that she is in reality his daughter-in-law—commanded that Gramont marry Lamira, a wealthy widow. Gramont and Felicia have a baby son who has just been kidnapped by pirates. Here, Gramont reacts to the news of his son's misfortune.

GRAMONT: Ha! what pains the fates are at to make a villain of me!
Must it be so? Shall I give up my honour
To save myself, and all I love from ruin?
No, that's in my own power, the rest in fate's,
And, spite of fate, I'll keep my honesty:
Tho' my best friend must be for me undone,
In fame, in fortune, and perhaps his life,
A sacrifice to treacherous revenge;
My infant by inhuman pirates murdered,
The dearest fruit of my Felicia's love;
My wife too, Oh my wife, she'll be thrown out
To wander through the world, poor, and distressed,
To curse her fatal love, to curse her husband,
The wretched source of bitterest miseries,
Who sees her starving, and can give no succour,
I cannot bear the thought, it shall not be;
I'd pluck those eyes out, rather than behold it.
So dear I hold her, I could cut off these limbs
To let her piece-meal feed upon my flesh.
I must, I must prevent at any rate
This dismal scene of misery and ruin,
Turn villain, any thing, when she's at stake,
My child too, and my best friend. I could, by Heav'n,
Suffer a thousand racking deaths for each,
And should I sacrifice 'em all, to keep

A little peace of mind, the pride of never straying?
Walk on by rules, and calmly let 'em perish,
Rather than tread one step beyond to save 'em?
Forbid it nature! No, I'll leap o'er all.
Castalio, my suffering babe and loved Felicia,
See how dear you're to me, how strong my love,
When it can turn the scale against my virtue.
Nay, now 'tis plain; not I, but fate resolves it.

The Iron Chest

George Coleman
1796

Scene: an English Manor

Dramatic

Mortimer: a man tortured by memories of the past, 30–40

Mortimer has murdered the uncle of Helen, the only woman he has ever loved. Here, the unhappy man confesses his deed to a faithful servant.

MORTIMER: Honour, thou blood-stain'd God! at whose red altar
Sit War and Homicide, O, to what madness
Will insult drive thy votaries! By heaven,
In the world's range there does not breathe a man
Whose brutal nature I more strove to soothe,
With long forbearance, kindness, courtesy,
Than his who fell by me. But he disgraced me,
Stain'd me,—oh, death, and shame! the world look'd on,
And saw this sinewy savage strike me down;
Rain blows upon me, drag me to and fro,
On the base earth, like carrion. Desperation,
In every fibre of my frame, cried vengeance!
I left the room, which he had quitted. Chance,
(Curse on the chance!) while boiling with my wrongs,
Thrust me against him, darkling in the street:—
I stab'd him to the heart:—and my oppressor
Roll'd, lifeless, at my foot.
[WILFORD: Oh! mercy on me!
How could this deed be cover'd!]
MORTIMER: Would you think it?
E'en at the moment when I gave the blow,
Butcher'd a fellow creature in the dark,
I had all good men's love. But my disgrace,
And my opponent's death, thus link'd with it,
Demanded notice of the magistracy.
They summon'd me, as friend would summon friend,
To acts of import, and communication.

We met: and 'twas resolved, to stifle rumour,
To put me on my trial. No accuser,
No evidence appear'd, to urge it on.—
'Twas meant to clear my fame.—How clear it, then?
How cover it? you say.—Why, by a Lie:—
Guilt's offspring, and its guard. I taught this breast,
Which Truth once made her throne, to forge a lie;
This tongue to utter it.—Rounded a tale,
Smooth as a Seraph's song from Satan's mouth;
So well compacted, that the o'er throng'd court
Disturb'd cool justice, in her judgment seat,
By shouting 'Innocence!' ere I had finish'd.
The Court enlarged me; and the giddy rabble
Bore me, in triumph, home. Aye!—look upon me.—
I know thy sight aches at me.
[*WILFORD:* Heaven forgive me!
I think I love you still:—but I am young,
I know not what to say:—it may be wrong.—
Indeed I pity you.]
MORTIMER: I disdain all pity.—
I ask no consolation. Idle boy!
Think'st thou that this compulsive confidence
Was given to move thy pity?—Love of Fame
(For still I cling to it) has urged me, thus,
To quash thy curious mischief in it's birth.
Hurt honour, in an evil, cursed hour,
Drove me to murder—lying:—'twould again.
My honesty,—sweet peace of mind,—all, all!
Are barter'd for a name. I *will* maintain it.
Should slander whisper o'er my sepulchre,
And my soul's agency survive in death,
I could embody it with heaven's lightning,
And the hot shaft of my insulted spirit
Should strike the blaster of memory
Dead in the church-yard. Boy, I would not kill thee:
Thy rashness and discernment threaten'd danger:
To check them there was no way left but this:—
Save one—your death:—you shall not be my victim.

Jean de France or
Hans Frandsen

Ludvig Holberg
1723

Scene: a village in Denmark

Serio-Comic
Jeronimus: a disgruntled citizen, 40–50

His daughter's fiancée has traveled to Paris, and Jeronimus objects to the lad's new pretentious Parisian mannerisms as they manifest in the letters that he sends home.

JERONIMUS: [Don't they all!] I don't know how he's living in Paris, but I know one thing: I don't like his letters at all! He calls my daughter Elsebet "Isabelle." He calls himself "Jean," and he calls me "Jerome"! He can call himself what he pleases. He can name himself Fairfax[10] or Sultan if he wants, as long as he calls my daughter and me by our Christian names!

[*FRANDSEN:* My dear neighbor, that's the style! Young men do that to show off that they've learned a foreign language.]

JERONIMUS: I don't dispute whether or not it's the style. I merely ask, is it a reasonable style? If a Frenchman named "Jean" visited this country and changed his name to "Hans" when he returned home, wouldn't his countrymen think he was crazy? It's a wonderful thing to learn a foreign language, but not until we've mastered our own; it's a wonderful thing to visit foreign countries, but not until we've gathered some years and maturity, not until we've earned enough capital to live on our interest; or to learn a profession we can't learn here at home. But here it's become some kind of right for poor middle-class children to go on such trips at random and destroy their families just to learn a language, which for just a few rix-dollars they can learn from a language teacher at home! Most of them get spoiled and learn nothing but crazy fashions and luxuriousness, which they bring back to infect the homeland, and forget the good that our schools taught them. I can name at least a dozen fine fellows who studied for the ministry and delivered sermons that earned them great respect, even in Our Lady's Church

[10]Fairfax: See *Jeppe of the Hill*, [Note: Sultan was also a popular dog's name.]

and Trinity Church, which have educated congregations. Those same boys, following the fashion, traveled abroad and, following the fashion, threw away their Christianity, right up to the Catechism, threw away their money, and brought back all sorts of strange political ideas. They walk around with their *Bonjour* and *Comment vous portez-vous*[11] starving themselves sick until they fall into melancholy and drunkenness! The parents see their children corrupted and themselves destroyed. So, go on and laugh at me, dear neighbor, but it's certainly true! If you saw all the money stacked in one place that our young people waste abroad every year, you wouldn't wonder why our country is so poor and powerless! Your son has already spent more than fifteen hundred rix-dollars in France. You say it's taught him to speak French, but you haven't said anything about how much Latin he's forgotten. The first thing he's learned are foolishness and madness! I can see them in the letters he's written to me. What the devil am I going to do with French letters that I don't understand a word of? First I have to pay postage; next I have to give Jan Baptist a bottle of wine to translate them into German; and then I can hardly understand them!

---

[11]*Bonjour*: good day. *Comment . . . vous*: how are you?

Jeppe of the Hill
Ludvig Holberg
1723

Scene: a village in Denmark

Serio-Comic
    Jeppe: a lazy ne'er-do-well. 30–40

> Jeppe has spent the morning shirking his responsibilities and here debates whether
> or not he should go home, or go back to the inn for another drink.

JEPPE: (*Alone. In a merry mood, he begins to sing.*)
A white hen and a speckled hen
Turned against a rooster . . .[12]

I wish I had the nerve to drink up another penny. Oh! I wish I had the
nerve to drink up another penny! I think I'll do it. No, I'll get in trouble.
If I could only get the inn out of my sight I wouldn't feel the need; but
it's like somebody's holding me back. I have to go in again. But what
are you doing, Jeppe? I see Nille, as though she's blocking the way with
Master Erich in her hand. I'll have to turn back. Oh, I wish I had the
nerve to drink up another penny! My belly says, "Do it." My back says,
"Don't." Which one should I cross? Isn't my belly more than my back? I
think so. Should I knock? Hey, Jacob Shoemaker, get out here! But that
damned woman blocks my way again. If she'd only hit my backbone so
it didn't hurt, I'd say to hell with it. But she hits like. . . . Oh, God
strengthen this poor man. What shall I do? Control your nature, Jeppe!
Isn't it disgraceful that you'd get yourself in trouble for a measly glass
of brandy? No! It won't happen this time. I must go on. Oh, I wish I had
the nerve to drink up another penny. It's my bad luck that I got that
first taste of it; now I can't leave. Move legs! The devil will tear you to
pieces if you don't go. No, the bastards won't budge at all. They want
to go to the inn again. My limbs are at war with each other; my belly
and legs want the inn and my back wants the town. Will you walk, you
dogs! You beasts! You rogues! No, damn them, they will go back to the
inn. I have more trouble getting my legs to walk away from the inn

---

[12]This song was supposedly a well-known drinking song containing satirical attacks on European royalty.

than I have getting my piebald horse out of the stable. Oh! I wish I had the nerve to drink up just one more single penny. Who knows, maybe Jacob Shoemaker will advance me a penny or two if I beg for it. Hey, Jacob! A glass of brandy for two pennies!

The Lancashire Witches

Thomas Shadwell
1682

Scene: England

Dramatic
   The Devil

   Here, the Devil tells his witches what they may expect in return for their loyalty.

DEVIL: At your command all Natures course shall cease,
And all the Elements make war or peace:
The Sky no more shall its known Laws obey,
Night shall retreat whilst you prolong the day.
Thy Charms shall make the Moon and Stars come down,
And in thick darkness hide the Sun at Noon.
Winds thou shalt raise, and streight their rage controul.
The Orbs upon their Axes shall not roll;
Hearing thy mighty Charms, the troubled sky
Shall crack with Thunder, Heav'n not knowing why.
Without one puff the Waves shall foam and rage,
Then though all Winds together should ingage,
The silent Sea shall not the Tempest feel.
Vallies shall roar, and trembling Mountains reel.
At thy command Woods from their seats shall rove.
Stones from their Quarries, and fixt Oaks remove
Vast standing lakes shall flow, and, at thy will,
The most impetuous Torrents shall stand still:
Swift Rivers shall (while wond'ring Banks admire)
Back to their Springs, with violent hast, retire.
Thy Charms shall blast full Fruits, and ripen'd Ears:
Ease anxious minds, and then afflict with cares.
Give Love, where Nature cannot, by thy skill,
And any living creature save or kill:
Raise Ghosts, transform your self, and whom you will.

The Learned Women

Molière
1672

Scene: Paris

Serio-Comic
> Chrysale: the head of a household of frustrating women, 40–50

> Chauvinism was alive and well in 17th century France as can be seen in the following speech delivered by the much harried Chrysale to his wife in which he condemns the emphasis she places on the education of their daughters.

CHRYSALE: Listen to me. I've got to make a scene,
Take off the mask at last, and vent my spleen.
Folks treat you both as mad, and if I knew . . .
[PHILAMINTE: How's that?]
CHRYSALE: I'm speaking now, sister, to you.
You wince at slips and solecisms in speech,
But your conduct displays plenty of each.
Your everlasting books, they please me not,
And should you burn the entire useless lot
—Except that Plutarch, where I keep my bands—
And leave your learning in the scholars' hands;
Should take out of the attic and my sight
That telescope that gives people a fright,
And all those knickknacks that would shame a loon;
Care not for what goes on up in the moon,
But what goes on here, in your residence,
Where nothing I can see makes any sense.
A woman should be willing to forego
The love of study and the lust to know.
To train her children's minds to be well-bred,
Manage the household, see that all are fed,
Control the servants, use economy:
This is her study, her philosophy.
In this respect our fathers were discerning
To say a woman has enough of learning
When her intellect, at its farthest reaches,

Can tell a doublet from a pair of breeches.
Their wives read nothing, but they lived full well;
Their households were the lore they had to tell,
Their books a thimble, needles, and some thread,
With which they made their daughter's clothes instead.
For today's women that is far too trite:
They want to become authors, they must write.
For them no science can be too profound;
And less so here than anywhere around;
For this is where the deepest thoughts are thought;
Here they know everything but what they ought.
They know the motion of the moon and stars
—A lot I care—of Venus, Saturn, Mars;
And with this vain, farfetched learning of theirs,
My pot goes unobserved and no one cares.
My help aspires to learning, to please you,
And leaves undone just what it ought to do;
My household reasons busily all day,
And reasoning drives reason far away:
One lets my roast burn while he reads some talc;
One dreams up verses when I call for ale;
In short, your fine example is observed,
And I have servants, and I am not served.
At least one serving-woman still was there
Not yet infected by this noxious air,
And so you kick her out with much *éclat*
Because she fails to speak good Vaugelas.
I tell you, I take all these things amiss
(It's to you, sister, I'm addressing this);
I don't like all your Latinizers here,
Especially Trissotin, whom you revere;
He it was ridiculed you both in verse;
All that he says is balderdash or worse;
After he speaks, you wonder what he said,
And I don't think he's quite right in the head.

The London Merchant or
The History of George Barnwell

George Lillo
1731

Scene: London

Dramatic
   Barnwell: a young man being manipulated by a scheming woman, 18

Barnwell's love for the unscrupulous Millwood has led him to embezzle money
from his employer and flee the city. Now the treacherous Millwood demands that
Barnwell murder his uncle. Here, the unhappy young man considers his options.

BARNWELL: A dismal gloom obscures the face of day; either the sun
has slipped behind a cloud, or journeys down the west of heaven, with
more than common speed, to avoid the sight of what I'm doomed to
act. Since I set forth on this accursed design, where'er I tread, methinks,
the solid earth trembles beneath my feet. Yonder limpid stream, whose
hoary fall has made a natural cascade, as I passed by, in doleful accents
seemed to murmur "Murder." The earth, the air, and water, seemed
concerned—but that's not strange; the world is punished, and nature
feels a shock when Providence permits a good man's fall! Just heaven!
Then what should I be? for him that was my father's only brother, and
since his death has been to me a father, who took me up an infant, and
an orphan; reared me with tenderest care, and still indulged me with
most paternal fondness—yet here I stand avowed his destined murderer. I stiffen with horror at my own impiety. 'Tis yet unperformed.
What if I quit my bloody purpose, and fly the place! (*Going, then stops.*)
But whither, oh whither, shall I fly? My master's once friendly doors
are ever shut against me; and without money Millwood will never see
me more, and life is not to be endured without her. She's got such firm
possession of my heart, and governs there with such despotic sway—
ay, there's the cause of all my sin and sorrow! 'Tis more than love; 'tis
the fever of the soul and madness of desire. In vain does nature, reason,
conscience, all oppose it; the impetuous passion bears down all before
it, and drives me on to lust, to theft, and murder. O conscience! feeble
guide to virtue, thou only show'st us when we go astray, but wantest
power to stop us in our course.—Ha, in yonder shady walk I see my

uncle. He's alone. Now for my disguise! (*Plucks out a vizor.*) This is his hour of private meditation. Thus daily he prepares his soul for heaven, whilst I—but what have I to do with heaven? Ha! No struggles, conscience!

Hence, hence, remorse, and ev'ry thought that's good!

The storm that lust began must end in blood.

(*Puts on the vizor, draws a pistol and exits.*)

The Misanthrope

Molière
1666

Scene: Paris

#1—Serio-Comic
   Alceste: the misanthrope, 30s

> When a trivial disagreement sparks an argument between Alceste and his friend, Philinte, the misanthrope reveals his utter contempt for people he describes as being "men of style."

ALCESTE: No, I cannot endure this fawning guile
Employed by nearly all your men of style.
There's nothing I so loathe as the gyrations
Of all these great makers of protestations,
These lavishers of frivolous embraces,
These utterers of empty commonplaces,
Who in civilities won't be outdone,
And treat the good man and the fool as one.
What joy is there in hearing pretty phrases
From one who loud and fulsome sings your praises,
Vows friendship, love, esteem for evermore,
Then runs to do the same to any boor?
No, no; a soul that is well constituted
Cares nothing for esteem so prostituted;
Our vanity is satisfied too cheap
With praise that lumps all men in one vast heap;
Esteem, if it be real, means preference,
And when bestowed on all it makes no sense.
Since these new vices seem to you so fine,
Lord! You're not fit to be a friend of mine.
I spurn the vast indulgence of a heart
That will not set merit itself apart;
No, singled out is what I want to be;
The friend of man is not the man for me.

Acaste: a self-assured Marquis, 20s

Here, the boastful Marquis takes a moment to sing his own praises

ACASTE: My word! When I regard myself, I find
No reason for despondency of mind.
I'm rich, I'm young, I'm of a family
With some pretention to nobility;
And through the rank that goes with my condition,
At court I can aspire to high position.
For courage, something we must all admire,
'Tis known I have been tested under fire,
And an affair of honor recently
Displayed my vigor and my bravery.
My wit is adequate, my taste discerning,
To judge and treat all subjects without learning;
When a new play is shown (which I adore),
To sit upon the stage, display my lore,
Determine its success, and stop the show
When any passage merits my "Bravo!"
I make a good appearance, rather chic;
I have fine teeth, an elegant physique.
And as for dress, all vanity aside,
My eminence can scarcely be denied.
I could not ask for more regard; I seem
To have the ladies' love, the King's esteem.
With all this, dear Marquis, I do believe
That no man anywhere has cause to grieve.

The Miser

Molière
1668

Scene: Paris

#1—Serio-Comic
> Maître Jacques: cook and coachman to the miser, any age

> When Harpagon, the miser, asks Maître Jacques to tell him what the people in town
> are saying about him, he is less than pleased with the servant's reply.

MAITRE JACQUES: Since you want it, sir, I'll tell you frankly that people everywhere make fun of you; that from every side they toss a hundred jokes at us on your account; and that they couldn't be more
delighted than in catching you with your pants down and telling stories constantly about your stinginess. One man says that you have spe-
cial almanacs printed in which you double the number of fast days and
vigils, so as to profit by the fasts that you force upon your household.
Another says that you always have a quarrel ready to pick with your
valets when it's time for presents or for them to leave you, so you can
find a reason for not giving them anything. This man tells how you
took the cat of one of your neighbors to court for having eaten up the
remains of a leg of lamb of yours. That man tells how you were caught
one night going, yourself, to steal your horses' oats; and that your
coachman, who was the one before me, in the dark, gave you I don't
know how many blows with a stick, which you never wanted to say
anything about. In short, do you want me to tell you how it is? A man
can't go anywhere he won't hear you hauled over the coals; you are a
byword and a laughingstock to everybody; and nobody ever speaks
about you except as a miser, skinflint, a pennypincher and a usurer.
[*HARPAGON:* (*Beating him.*) You are a numbskull, a rogue, and an im-
pudent scoundrel.]
MAITRE JACQUES: Well! Didn't I guess right? You wouldn't believe
me. I told you I'd make you angry if I told you the truth.

#2—Serio-Comic
    Harpagon: a foolish miser, 40–50

Harpagon lives a Scrooge-like existence and guards his possessions with paranoid zeal. When he is robbed of his most precious treasure chest, he falls into a great panic.

HARPAGON: (Shouting "Stop, thief!" from the garden, and coming in without his hat.) Stop, thief! Stop, thief! Assassin! Murderer! Justice, just Heaven! I'm ruined, I'm assassinated, they've cut my throat, they've stolen my money. Who can it be? What has become of him? Where is he? Where is he hiding? What shall I do to find him? Which way shall I run? Which way shall I not run? Isn't he here? Isn't he here? Who is it? Stop! *(Catches his own arm.)* Give me back my money, you scoundrel. . . . Oh, it's me. My mind is troubled, and I don't know where I am, who I am, or what I'm doing. Alas! My poor money, my poor money, my dear friend! They've deprived me of you; and since you are taken from me, I've lost my support, my consolation, my joy; all is finished for me, and there's nothing more for me to do in the world; without you, it's impossible for me to live. It's all over, I can't go on; I'm dying, I'm dead, I'm buried. Isn't there anyone who will bring me back to life by giving me back my dear money, or by telling me who took it? Eh? What do you say? . . . It's no one. Whoever it was that did it, he must have watched his opportunity with great care; and he chose just the time when I was talking to my traitor of a son. Let's go out; I'm going to fetch the law, and have everyone in my house put to the torture: maidservants, valets, son, daughter, and myself too. *(Looking at the audience.)* What a lot of people assembled! There's no one my eyes light on but gives me suspicions, and everyone looks like a thief. Eh? What are they talking about over there? About the man who robbed me? What's that noise they're making up there? Is my thief there? For Heaven's sake, if anyone has any news of my thief, I implore him to tell me. Isn't he hiding there among you? . . . They're all looking at me and laughing. You'll see, beyond a doubt they're all involved in my robbery. Let's go, quick, officers, policemen, provosts, judges, racks, gallows, and executioners. I'll have everybody hanged; and if I don't find my money, I'll hang myself afterward.

The Mistake

Sir John Vanbrugh
1705

Scene: Spain

Serio-Comic
Sancho: a foolish servant, 20–30

> When he and his master are both slighted by the women they love, Sancho delivers
> the following misogynistic observation of the fairer sex.

SANCHO: True, we are Men; boo—Come, Master, let us both be in a
passion; here's my Scepter. (*Shewing a Cudgel.*) Subject *Jacinta*, look
about you. Sir, was you ever in *Muscovy?* the Women there love the
Men dearly, why? because,—(*Shaking his Stick.*) there's your Love-pow-
der, for you. Ah, Sir, were we but Wise and Stout, what work shou'd
we make with 'em: But this humble Love-making spoils 'em all. A rare
way indeed to bring Matters about with 'em; we are persuading 'em all
Day they are Angels and Goddesses, in order to use 'em at Night like
human Creatures; we are like to succeed truly.

[*DON CAR.:* For my part, I never yet cou'd bear a Slight from any
Thing, nor will I now. There's but one Way however to resent it from a
Woman; and that's to drive her bravely from your Heart, and place a
worthier in her vacant Throne.]

SANCHO: Now with Submission to my Betters, I have another way,
Sir; I'll drive my Tyrant from my Heart, and place my self in her
Throne. Yes: I will be Lord of my own Tenement, and keep my Housh-
old in Order. Wou'd you wou'd do so too, Master; for look you, I have
been Servitor in a Colledge at *Salamancha*, and read Philosophy with
the Doctors; where I found that a Woman in all Times has been ob-
serv'd to be an Animal hard to understand, and much inclin'd to Mischief. Now, as an Animal is always an Animal, and a Captain always a
Captain, so a Woman is always a Woman: Whence it is that a certain
Greek says, Her Head is like a Bank of Sand; or as another, A solid
Rock; or according to a Third, A Dark Lanthorn. Pray Sir, observe; for
this is close Reasoning; and so, as the Head is the Head of the Body;
and that the Body without a Head, is like a Head without a tail; and
that where there is neither Head nor Tail 'tis a very strange Body: So I
say a Woman is by Comparison; do you see; (for nothing explains

things like Comparisons) I say by Comparison, as *Aristotle* has often said before me, one may compare her to the raging Sea; for as the Sea, when the Wind rises, knits its Brows like any angry Bull, and that Waves mount upon Rocks, and Rocks mount upon Waves; that Porpusses leap like Trouts, and Whales skip about like Gudgeons; that Ships rowl like Beer-Barrels, and Mariners pray like Saints; just so I say a Woman—A Woman, I say, just so, when her Reason is Ship-wrack'd upon her Passion, and the Hulk of her Understanding lies thumping against the Rock of her Fury; then it is I say, that by certain Immotions, which—um—cause, as one may suppose, a sort of Convulsive,—yes—Hurricanious—um—Like in short; a Woman, is like the Devil, Sir.

The Mourning Bride
William Congreve
1697

Scene: Granada

Dramatic
        Gonsalez: a a sycophant, 40–50

Gonsalez wishes the Princess of Granada to marry his son. Here, he greets the young lady in the palace, and in as flowery a manner as possible, tells her of her father's return from doing battle with the Moors.

GONSALEZ: Be ev'ry day of your long life like this.
The fun, bright conquest, and your brighter eyes,
Have all conspir'd to blaze promiscuous light,
and bless this day with most unequal lustre.
Your royal father, my victorious lord,
Loaden with spoils, and ever-living laurel,
Is ent'ring now, in martial pomp, the palace.
Five hundred mules precede his solemn march,
Which groan beneath the weight of Moorish wealth.
Chariots of war, adorn'd with glitt'ring gems,
Succeed; and next, a hundred neighing steeds,
White as the fleecy rain on Alpine hills;
That bound and foam, and champ the golden bit,
As they disdain'd the victory they grace.
Prisoners of war in shining fetters follow:
And captains of the noblest blood of Afric
Sweat by his chariot-wheels, 'and lick and grind,
With gnashing teeth, the dust his triumphs raise.'
The swarming populace spread every wall,
'And cling, as if with claws they did enforce
Their hold, thro' clifted stones, stretching and staring,
As if they were all eyes, and every limb
Would feed its faculty of admiration.'
While you alone retire and shun this fight!
This fight, which is indeed not seen (tho' twice
The multitude should gaze) in absence of your eyes.

Nathan the Wise

Gotthold Ephrain Lessing
1779

Scene: Jerusalem

Dramatic

Knight: a young Knight Templar, 20s

Despite himself, this young Knight Templar has fallen in love with a Jewess. Here, he agonizes over his impossible passion while awaiting the young lady's father.

TEMPLAR: (*Walks up and down, struggling with himself, till he breaks out.*)
Here halts the victim, weary and foredone—
'Tis well! I would not know or see more clear
What in me passes, and would not foresee
What yet will pass. Enough! I've fled in vain,
In vain! And yet I could nought else but fly.
Well, come what will; the stroke fell far too swiftly
To be escaped; though hard and long I struggled
To come from under. To see her, whom yet
To see I had but small desire, to see her
And the resolve never to lose her from
Mine eyes, and yet what speak I of resolve?
Resolve is plan, is act, while I but suffer,
Suffer, not act—to see her and to feel
Bound to her by strong cords, bound up with her,
Was one; is one: from her to live apart
Is thought unthinkable and were my death,
And wheresoever after death we are,
'Twould be even there my death—Is this, then, love?
So the Knight Templar loves assuredly,
The Christian loves the Jewish maid, in truth;
Hm! what of that? In this Holy Land,
And hereby holy to me evermore,
I have sloughed off a world of prejudices,—
What will my Order say? As Templar Knight
I'm dead, was dead to them from that self hour
Which made me prisoner to Saladin,—

The head which Saladin restored to me,
Was it my old?—'tis new! and clear of all
The lies and stuff they babbled to it once,
Wherewith 'twas slaved; and 'tis a better one,
Agreeing more with my paternal clime,
I feel it so in truth. For it begins
To think even as my father must have thought
Under those skies, unless those tales be false
They tell of him—Tales? tales, yet credible
Which never seemed to me more credible
Than here they seem where I but run the risk
Of stumbling, where he fell. Ah, where he fell?
I'll rather fall with men, than stand with children.
Sure, his example makes me confident
Of his approval. Whose approval else crave I?
For Nathan's? Furtherance more than approval
Will not be wanting there. The noble Jew!
Who yet desires not to seem more than Jew!
Here comes he hastening, gladness in his eyes.
Whoe'er came otherwise from Saladin?
Ho! Nathan!

Pizarro

Richard Brinsley Sheridan
1799

Scene: Peru

Dramatic

Las-Casas: an older General in the Spanish Army occupying Peru, 50s

When Pizarro and his bloodthirsty men call for battle with the Incans, Las-Casas makes a plea for peace.

LAS-CASAS: Is then the dreadful measure of your cruelty not yet compleat?—Battle!—gracious Heaven! Against whom?—Against a King, in whose mild bosom your atrocious injuries even yet have not excited hate! but who, insulted or victorious, still sues for peace. Against a People who never wronged the living Being their Creator formed: a People, who, children of innocence received you as cherish'd guests with eager hospitality and confiding kindness. Generously and freely did they share with you their comforts, their treasures, and their homes: you repaid them by fraud, oppression, and dishonour. These eyes have witnessed all I speak—as Gods you were received; as Fiends have you acted.[13]

[PIZARRO: Las-Casas!]

LAS-CASAS: Pizarro, hear me!—Hear me, chieftains!—And thou, Allpowerful! whose thunders can shiver into sand the adamantine rock—whose lightnings can pierce to the core of the rived and quaking earth—Oh! let thy power give effect to thy servant's words, as thy spirit gives courage to his will! Do not, I implore you, Chieftains—Countrymen—Do not, I implore you, renew the foul barbarities which your insatiate avarice has inflicted on this wretched, unoffending race!—But hush, my sighs—fall not, drops of useless sorrow!—heart-breaking anguish, choke not my utterance—All I entreat is, send me once more to those you *call* your enemies—Oh! let me be the messenger of penitence from you, I shall return with blessings and with peace from them.—

[13] 'The speech of this good old Priest is one of the finest and most impressive in the whole Piece...' (*The Oracle*, 25 May 1799). Harvard MS. fms Thr 5 reads: 'What a dreadful reflexion! a Battle—against whom? against a king, that a few days ago offered peace—against a nation, that in innocence, and with purity worship their Creator in their accustomed way and manner.'

Elvira, you weep!—Alas! and does this dreadful crisis move no heart but thine?

[*ALMAGRO:* Because there are no women here but she and thou.

PIZARRO: Close this idle war of words: time flies, and our opportunity will be lost. Chieftains, are ye for instant battle?

[*ALL:* We are]

LAS-CASAS: Oh, men of blood!—(*Kneels.*) God! thou hast anointed me thy servant—not to curse, but to bless my countrymen: yet now my blessing on their force were blasphemy against thy goodness.—(*Rises.*) No! I curse your purpose, homicides! I curse the bond of blood by which you are united. May fell division, infamy, and rout, defeat your projects and rebuke your hopes! On you, and on your children, be the peril of the innocent blood which shall be shed this day! I leave you, and for ever! No longer shall these aged eyes be feared by the horrors they have witnessed. In caves, in forests, will I hide myself: with Tigers and with savage beasts will I commune: and when at length we meet again before the bless'd tribunal of that Deity, whose mild doctrines and whose mercies ye have this day renounced, then shall YOU feel the agony and grief of soul which tear the bosom of your accuser now! (*Going.*)

Phèdre

Jean Racine
1677

Scene: Trezene: a city in the Pelopannesos

Dramatic

Hippolyte: son of Theseus, 20–30

Hippolyte is a stern young man who has disavowed love. When he meets the captive princess, Aricie, however, his resolve begins to waver and confusion sets in. When his old friend and tutor asks him whether or not he's fallen in love with the young woman, he offers the following reply.

HIPPOLYTE: How can you use that word?
You, who have known my heart since first my spirit stirred—
a heart that only knows such distance and disdain,
a heart that hardly can return to earth again.
Son of an Amazon, I drank her milk and drew
that strong and stubborn pride which seems to baffle you;
considering myself, the way a young man does,
I gave myself great praise when I knew who I was.
You who were close to me, who saw to all my needs,
you made me learn by heart my famous father's deeds.
You told me of his life, and once you had begun,
I was on fire to hear whatever he had done:
So you described the way this hero had consoled
mankind for its great loss of Hercules, and told
me how he slew Sinnis, told how he killed Scirron,
and destroyed Procrustes, and slaughtered Cercyon,
took Epidaurus' bones and spilled them in the mud,
then covered over Crete with Minotaur's life blood,
But when you told of deeds that sounded more like crimes,
how Theseus used to break his word a hundred times—
Helen is raped away from Sparta by his lies;
poor Salamis must sit as Periboëa cries—
and there were many more whose names escape me now,
who loved him, and believed that he would keep his vow:
Ariadne, weeping in silence by the sea,
Phèdre, too, whom he seduced, although more happily;

ah, you remember how I begged you to be brief,
such stories made me grave, they stayed and gave me grief;
if it were in my will to wrench them from my brain
so only the brave deeds and glories would remain!
Could I be so enslaved and waste my life away?
Could some god make me cheat, dissemble and betray?
Loose and lascivious, I would twice the shame
of Theseus—I have none of his great claim to fame
no name, and no strange beasts defeated, and no right
to fail as he has failed, or fall from his steep height.
And yet suppose my pride should mellow and grow mild,
why should it be for this Aricie, this child?
Surely I sense, deep in the darkness of my heart,
there is a law that says we two must stay apart?
My father disapproves, and by a stern decree,
forbids that she enlarge her brother's family:
he fears some bright new life from that guilt-ridden line,
therefore each leaf must wilt, and so die on the vine.
This sister must stay chaste forever to the tomb
and bury their bad name in her own barren womb.
Should I stand by her side against my father's laws?
Show off my arrogance by taking up her cause?
Should I let love set sail the madness of my youth . . .

The Political Tinker

Ludvig Holberg
1722

Scene: Hamburg

#1—Serio-Comic
Henrich: a helpful servant, 40–50

When young Antonious arrives to ask for his mistress' hand in marriage, Henrich gives the lad advice than takes a moment to recall the time he proposed.

HENRICH: (*Alone.*) The most difficult part of proposing is to figure out the right way to begin speaking; I decided to propose once myself, but after fourteen days I still couldn't figure out what to say! I knew well enough that I should begin my speech with either "whereas" or "inasmuch as"; the trouble was that I couldn't figure out the other words to stick on that "whereas." I didn't feel like troubling myself any longer with it, so I went and bought a speech from Jacob Schoolmaster for eight pennies, for he sells speeches for that. But it went like hell for me. When I got right in the middle of my speech I couldn't remember the rest, and I was too ashamed to take the paper out of my pocket. I could recite that speech both before and after as perfectly as the Lord's Prayer, but when I tried to use it for real, the words stuck in my throat. It went like this: "After official greetings and salutations—I, Henrich Andersen, am come hither with the purpose, intent, and resolve to inform thee that I am no more without feelings than others; and whereas as all things in the world find themselves love, including dumb beasts, even I with God and propriety, am come hither unworthily to desire and ask thee to be my heart's truest love." If someone will give me back my eight pennies, I'll hand it over. It's honestly worth the money; for I believe that whoever speaks in this manner can get any respectable man's daughter that he wants. But here comes the master, I have to run!

Herman: a foolish man with political aspirations, 40–50

Herman wastes no opportunity to publicly criticize the city council and has consequently drawn their fire. In order to punish pompous Herman, the council conceives a plot in which they tell Herman he has been declared Burgomaster. It is their belief that a simpleton like Herman will soon crack under the strain of command. Here, an ecstatic Herman tells his wife and servant how their lives will change now that he is Burgomaster.

HERMAN: Nonsense! When I'm not home, you must answer, "Mr. Burgomaster von Bremenfeld is not home"; and when I don't want to be bothered you'll say, "The burgomaster is not granting audience today." Listen, Sweetheart, you must quickly make some coffee, you have to have something to offer the councilmen's wives when they arrive; for from now on our reputation will be, that people can say, "Burgomaster von Bremenfeld gives good advice, and his wife good coffee." I'm so afraid, Sweetheart, that you'll do something wrong before you become used to your new position. Henrich, run and get a tea table and some cups and let the maid run after four pennies worth of coffee; we can always buy more later. For the time being, it must be the rule, Sweetheart, that you say as little as possible until you learn genteel conversation. You mustn't be too humble, either, but stand up for your respect, and do everything you can to get the old pewterer ways out of your head and make believe that you've been a burgomaster's wife for many years. Every morning there must always be a table prepared with tea for the visitors who come, in the afternoon a table prepared with coffee, and after that we play cards. The card game they play is Allumber; I'd give a hundred rix-dollars if you and our daughter, Engelke, understood it. You must pay careful attention when the others play, so you can catch on! In the mornings you must lounge in bed until nine or nine-thirty, for only common people get up in the summer with the sun; excepting on Sundays, when you must get up earlier because that's when I take my laxative. You must get a beautiful snuffbox, which you set on the table when you play cards. When someone drinks to your health, you don't say, "Thanks," but instead, *"Très humble Servitör."* And when you yawn, don't cover your mouth, for that is no longer done among distinguished people, finally, when you're in company, don't be too proper, but put off your propriety a little. . . . Listen, I forget something: You must also get yourself a lapdog, which you shall love as much as your own daughter; for that's also fashionable. Our neighbor's wife, Arianke, has a cute dog that she'll surely lend you until we can get our own. You must give the dog a French name, that I'll come up with when I get some time to think about it. It should always lie in your lap, and you must kiss it at least half a dozen times when visitors are here.[14]

[*GESKE:* No, my dear husband, I can't possibly do that; for you don't always know where a dog has lain and dirtied itself. On top of that, you could get either a mouthful of filth or fleas.]

HERMAN: No nonsense! If you're going to be a lady, then you must act like a lady. Such a dog can also give you opportunities for conversation; for when you can't think of anything to say, you can talk about your dog's qualities and virtues. Just do as I say, Sweetheart. I understand the fashionable world better than you. Just mirror me. You'll see that there won't be the slightest remains of the old lifestyle left in me. It won't happen to me like it happened to a certain butcher who became councilman. When he finished writing one page and had to turn the sheet, he put his pen in his mouth, like he used to do with his butcher knife. You go in now and prepare; I have to talk to Henrich a little, alone.

---

[14]Allumber was a popular card game brought to Denmark by Just Høgh about 1690. The name is derived from the French '*L ombre. Très humble sèrvitör:* "most respectful servant." Geske should have said "*très humble servante.*"

The Prince of Parthia

Thomas Godfrey
1767

Scene: Ctesiphon

Dramatic

    Vardanes: the Prince of Parthia, 20s

    Here, sullen Vardanes reveals his hatred of his brother, Arsaces, who is the King's favorite.

VARDANES: I hate *Arsaces*,
Tho' he's my Mother's son, and churchmen say
There's something sacred in the name of Brother.
My soul endures him not, and he's the bane
Of all my hopes of greatness. Like the sun
He rules the day, and like the night's pale Queen,
My fainter beams are lost when he appears.
And this because he came into the world,
A moon or two before me: What's the diff'rence,
That he alone should shine in Empire's seat?
I am not apt to trumpet forth my praise.
Or highly name myself, but this I'll speak,
To him in ought, I'm not the least inferior.
Ambition, glorious fever! mark of Kings,
Gave me immortal thirst and rule of Empire.
Why lag'd my tardy soul, why droop'd the wing,
Nor forward springing, shot before his speed
To seize the prize?—'Twas Empire—
Oh! 't was Empire—

The Projectors

John Wilson
1664

Scene: London

Serio-Comic

    Leanchops: the beleaguered servant of a miser, any age

    Leanchops works for the most miserly gentlemen in London. Here, he complains
bitterly of his employers thrift.

LEANCHOPS: Well! o' my conscience there was never so unlucky a fellow as myself! Service, do you call it? Certainly, if damnation be only
pœna sensus, that were a fitter name for it! Here I live with a master that
has wealth enough; but so fearful, sad, pensive, suspicious a fellow,
that he disquiets both himself and every one else! Art, I have heard say,
has but seven liberal sciences, but he has a thousand illiberal! There
lives not a more base, niggardly, unsatiable pinchpenny, nor a more
gaping, gripping, polling,[15] extorting, devouring cormorant! A sponge
sucks not up faster, and yet a pumice gives back easier! The sign is always with him in the clutches; and a kite's pouncke truss[16] not more
readily! He shall watch you a young heir as diligently as a raven a
dying horse, and yet swallow him with more tears than a crocodile! He
never sleeps but he seals up the nose of his bellows, lest they lose
breath, and has almost broke his brains to find the like device for his
chimney and his throat! A gamester has not studied the advantage of
dice half so much as he a sordid parsimony, which yet he calls thrift;
and will tell you to a crumb how much difference there is in point of
loss between a hundred dozen of bread broken with the hand and cut
with a knife! The devil's in him, and I am as weary of him as of our last
journey, which both of us perform'd on the same horse! As thus:—In
the morning, about two hours before him, out gets Peel Garlick, he jogs
after, overtakes me, rides through the next town and a little beyond it,
leaves palfrey agrazing for me and marches on himself. In like manner I
get up, overtake him, ride on, leave him on this side of the next town,

---

[15]Thieving, cheating.

[16]Pouncke—*i.e.* 'pounces,'—the talons or claws of a bird of prey. 'Trussing,' in falconry, is
the hawk soaring up with any fowl or prey, and then descending with it.

and so order our business, that he rides out in the morning and into the inn at night, and through every town by the way. Nor need we fear any man's stealing him! Smithfield, at the end of a long vacation, can't show such another wall-ey'd, crestfallen, saddle-back'd, flat-ribbed, gut-founder'd, shoulder-pitch'd, spur-gall'd, hip-shotten, grease-moulton jade, besides splint, spavin, glanders, farce, stringhalt, sprains, scratches, malander, and wind-galls innumerable! Like the fool's hobbyhorse, were it not for the name of a horse a man had as lief go afoot; and thus we jog on in grief together. But hold! I hear him—somewhat's amiss!

The Provoked Wife

Sir John Vanbrugh
1697

Scene: England

Serio-Comic
  Sir John Brute: a man chafing in his marriage, 20–30

  Sir John can no longer tolerate his wife, as he here so eloquently states.

SIR JOHN: What cloying meat is love, when matrimony's the sauce to it. Two years' marriage has debauched my five senses. Everything I see, everything I hear, everything I feel, everything I smell, and everything I taste, methinks has wife in't. No boy was ever so weary of his tutor, no girl of her bib, no nun of doing penance, nor old maid of being chaste, as I am of being married. Sure there's a secret curse entailed upon the very name of wife. My lady is a young lady, a fine lady, a witty lady, a virtuous lady, and yet I hate her. There is but one thing on earth I loathe beyond her: that's fighting. Would my courage come up but to a fourth part of my ill nature, I'd stand buff to her relations, and thrust her out of doors. But marriage has sunk me down to such an ebb of resolution, I dare not draw my sword, though even to get rid of my wife. But here she comes.

The Rivals

Richard Brinsley Sheridan
1775

Scene: Bath

Serio-Comic
> Faulkner: a young man in love, 20s

> Faulkner and Julia are bound to marry by contract. When Faulkner questions her love for him, she leaves in tears. Here, the unhappy young man calls after her.

FAULKNER: In tears! Stay, Julia: stay but for a moment.—The door is fastened! Julia!—my soul—but for one moment. I hear her sobbing! 'Sdeath! what a brute am I to use her thus! Yet stay!—Aye—she is coming now. How little resolution there is in woman! How a few soft words can turn them!—No, faith!—she is *not* coming either! Why, Julia—my love—say but that you forgive me—come but to tell me that. Now, this is being *too* resentful.—Stay! she *is* coming too—I thought she would—no *steadiness* in anything! her going away must have been a mere trick then. She sha'nt see that I was hurt by it. I'll affect indifference. (*Hums a tune: then listens.*)—No—Z—ds! she's *not* coming!—nor don't intend it, I suppose. This is not *steadiness*, but *obstinacy!* Yet I deserve it. What, after so long an absence to quarrel with her tenderness!—'twas barbarous and unmanly! I should be ashamed to see her now. I'll wait till her just resentment is abated—and when I distress her so again, may I lose her forever, and be linked instead to some antique virago, whose gnawing passions, and long-hoarded spleen shall make me curse my folly half the day, and all the night!

The Rovers

George Canning, John Hookman Frere, and George Ellis
1798

Scene: A subterraneous vault

Serio-Comic
> Rogero: a captive knight, 30s

> Rogero has been held prisoner for eleven years. Here, he wanders his underground
> gaol and thinks of Matilda, his one true love.

ROGERO: Eleven years! it is now eleven years since I was first im-
mured in this living sepulchre—the cruelty of a Minister—the perfidy
of a Monk—yes, Matilda! for thy sake—alive amidst the dead—
chained—coff'ned—confined—cut off from the converse of my fellow-
men.—Soft!—what have we here? (*Stumbles over a bundle of sticks.*) This
cavern is so dark, that I can scarcely distinguish the objects under my
feet. Oh!—the register of my captivity—Let me see, how stands the account? (*Takes up the sticks, and turns them over with a melancholy air; then
stands silent for a few moments, as if absorbed in calculation.*) eleven years
and fifteen days!—Hah! the twenty-eighth of August! How does the
recollection of it vibrate on my heart! It was on this day that I took my
last leave of Matilda. It was a summer evening—her melting hand
seemed to dissolve in mine, as I prest it to my bosom—Some demon
whispered me that I should never see her more.—I stood gazing on the
hated vehicle which was conveying her away for ever.—The tears were
petrified under my eyelids.—My heart was crystallized with agony.—
Anon—I looked along the road.—The Diligence seemed to diminish
every instant.—I felt my heart beat against its prison, as if anxious to
leap out and overtake it.—My soul whirled 'round as I watched the ro-
tation of the hinder wheels.—A long trail of glory followed after her,
and mingled with the dust.—it was the emanation of Divinity, lumi-
nous with love and beauty—like the splendour of the setting sun—but
it told me that the sun of my joys was sunk for ever—Yes, here in the
depths of an eternal dungeon—in the nursing cradle of hell—the sub-
urbs of perdition—in a nest of demons, where despair in vain sits
brooding over the putrid eggs of hope; where agony woes the embrace
of death; where patience, beside the bottomless pool of despondency,

sits angling for impossibilities—Yet even *here*, to behold her, to embrace her—Yes, Matilda, whether in this dark abode, amidst toads and spiders, or in a royal palace, amidst the more loathsome reptiles of a Court, would be indifferent to me—Angels would shower down their hymns of gratulation upon our heads—while fiends would envy the eternity of suffering love. . . . Soft, what air was that? it seemed a sound of more than human warblings—Again (*Listens attentively for some minutes.*)—Only the wind—It is well, however—it reminds me of that melancholy air, which has so often solaced the hours of my captivity—Let me see whether the damps of this dungeon have not yet injured my guitar. (*Takes his Guitar, tunes it, and begins the following Air with a full accompaniment of Violins from the Orchestra.*) (*Air, Lanterna Magica.*)

The School for Scandal

Richard Brinsley Sheridan
1777

Scene: London

Serio-Comic

Sir Peter Teazle: an exasperated husband, 40s

Sir Peter married a country woman much younger than he in hopes of sharing his life with someone as yet untainted by material desires. When his wife quickly adapts to city ways, he finds himself at his wits' end.

SIR PETER: When an old bachelor takes a young wife, what is he to expect?—'Tis now six months since Lady Teazle made me the happiest of men—and I have been the miserablest dog ever since that ever committed wedlock! We tift a little going to church, and came to a quarrel before the bells were done ringing. I was more than once nearly choked with gall during the honeymoon, and had lost all comfort in life before my friends had done wishing me joy! Yet I chose with caution—a girl bred wholly in the country, who never knew luxury beyond one silk gown, nor dissipation above the annual gala of a race ball. Yet now she plays her part in all the extravagent fopperies of the fashion and the town, with as ready a grace as if she had never seen a bush nor a grass-plat out of Grosvenor Square! I am sneered at by my old acquaintance—paragraphed in the newspapers. She dissipates my fortune, and contradicts all my humors; yet the worst of it is, I doubt I love her, or I should never bear all this. However, I'll never be weak enough to own it.

The Scowrers

Thomas Shadwell
1691

Scene: London

Dramatic
    Mr. Rant: a concerned father, 50–60

Mr. Rant is distressed about his proligate son's drunken lifestyle. Here, he finally takes the youth to task.

MR. RANT: Heaven turn your heart:
I am glad at least, you appear so much asham'd,
For Shame for Faults is one good step to Wisdom;
But what hope can I have, that one short Moment
Can make you turn from your long course of Lewdness,
Such Lewdness as I am asham'd to think of:
Such mean, such foolish Lewdness as has made
Your Name too scandalous for a civil Mouth,
When but even now I saw you in your Pranks—
[SIR WILLIAM: Tis the last time.]
MR. RANT: Till wicked drink possesses you again,
That bane to Vertue and to common Sense,
That makes you live in a continued Mist,
Without the benefit of one clear thought;
Nature has prudently contrived each Man,
In the worst miseries of humane Life
Would be himself, and I would be I still,
But sordid Drunkenness makes you differ more
From your lov'd self, than from another Man.
[SIR WILLIAM: You rouse me, Sir, out of a Lethargy.]
MR. RANT: Ye think your selves the finest Gentlemen,
When you are most to be despised or pitty'd,
Not Monkeys can be more ridiculous,
Besides the Infamy you most contract,
In the opinion of the good and wise,
As soon I'd choose a Madman for a Friend,
You vomit secrets, when o'recharg'd with Wine,

You often quarrel with the best of Friends:
And she must be bold as is a Lioness,
Who takes you for a Husband: Drink in short
Provokes you to all Folly, to all Vice,
Till you become a Nusance to Mankind;
You'll say they are men of Wit, but have a care
Of a great Wit, who has no Understanding.
[*SIR WILLIAM:* You speak, Sir, like an Oracle.]
MR. RANT: By Drunkenness you are useless at the best,
Unless as Flys or humble Bees, meer Drones.
What Office is there in a Common-wealth,
A Drunkard can sustain? Unless it be one,
To be a Strainer through which Claret runs.
Your Nerves you weaken, and you drown your Minds;
You're all meer Sops in Wine, your Brains are Bogs;
A Toast is equal to a common Drunkard:
You'll say you have Courage, No, it is not Valour;
Valour is joyn'd with Vertue, never prostitute,
But sacred, and employ'd to just Defence.
Of Prince and Country, and the best of Friends,
With necessary vindication of our Honour:
Yours is a brutal Fierceness that annoys
Mankind, and makes 'em fear and hate you too.
[*SIR WILLIAM:* These are unanswerable Truths.]
MR. RANT: The use of common Whores is most pernicious,
By which, the least you venture is your Nose,
And private ones you cannot gain, without
Being a most perfidious Knave, and striking
At the very Root of all Morality.
Have I with such Tenderness bred you up?
With such great care and vast Expence, infused
Whatever you were capable of receiving,
Taught you all Arts that could adorn a Gentleman:
None with such care could cultivate a Plant.
[*SIR WILLIAM:* All this with humble Gratitude I confess.]
MR. RANT: Heaven had endued you with sufficient Wit
And Parts, and you, in spight of these Advantages,

Which might have made you famous in your Country,
To make your self lewd, even to a Proverb!
Is this your sence of Honour, and is this
Your Gratitude to me, after such great Indulgence,
Such good Advice, such tender Love, as I
Have so long shew'd you? You have so often
Set my Eyes on flowing, that I have wondered
Whence the Moysture came that could supply them.

Tancred and Sigismunda

James Thompson, Esq.
@1730

Scene: Palermo, Sicily

Dramatic
      Osmond: Lord High Constable of Sicily, 20–30

> Osmond has been granted the Lord Chancellor's daughter's hand in marriage.
> When Sigismunda is informed that she will marry Osmond, she collapses in despair.
> Here, Osmond reacts to Sigismunda's rejection of his suit and subsequently becomes
> determined to have her for himself.

OSMOND: (*Alone.*) Let me think—
What can this mean?—Is it to me aversion?
Or is it, as I feared, she loves another?
Ha!—yes—perhaps the king, the young count *Tancred!*
They were bred up together—Surely that,
That cannot be—Has he not given his hand,
In the most solemn manner, to *Constantia?*
Does not his crown depend upon the deed?
'No—if they lov'd, and this old statesman knew it,
He could not to a king prefer a subject.
His virtues I esteem—nay more, I trust them—
So far as virtue goes—but could he place
His daughter on the throne of *Sicily*—
O 'tis a glorious bribe, too much for man!'—
What is it then?—I care not what it be.
'My honour now, my dignity demands,
That my propos'd alliance, by her father,
And even herself accepted, be not scorn'd.
I love her too—I never knew till now
To what a pitch I lov'd her. O she shot
Ten thousand charms into my inmost soul!
She look'd so mild, so amiably gentle,
She bow'd her head, she glow'd with such confusion,
Such loveliness of modesty! She is,
In gracious mind, in manners, and in person,
The perfect model of all female beauty!'

She must be mine—She is!—If yet her heart
Consents not to my happiness, her duty,
Join'd to my tender cares, will gain so much
Upon her generous nature—That will follow.
The man of sense, who acts a prudent part,
Not flattering steals, but forms himself the heart.

Three Hours after Marriage

John Gay
@1720

Scene: London

Serio-Comic
> Fossile: a newlywed, 30s

> A mere three hours after the wedding ceremony, Fossile intercepts a suggestive note addressed to his new bride, and is here horrified that she may be in love with someone else.

FOSSILE: There are now no more Secrets between us. Man and Wife are One.

> *Madam, Either I mistake the Encouragement I have had, or I am to be happy to-Night. I hope the same Person will compleat her good Offices: I stand to Articles. The Ring is a fine one; and I shall have the Pleasure of putting it on for the first time.*
> *This from your impatient, R. P.*

In the name of Beelzebub, what is this? *Encouragement! Happy to-Night! same Person! good Offices!* Whom hast thou married, poor *Fossile?* Couldst thou not divert thyself still with the Spoils of Quarries and Coal-pits, thy Serpents and thy Salamanders, but thou must have a living Monster too! 'Sdeath! what a Jest shall I be to our Club! Is there no Rope among my Curiosities? Shall I turn her out of doors, and proclaim my infamy; or lock her up, and bear my Misfortunes? Lock her up! Impossible. One may shut up Volatile Spirits, pen up the Air, confine Bears, Lyons and Tygers, nay, keep even your Gold: But a Wanton Wife who can keep?

The Tragedy of Zara

Aaron Hill, Esq.

@1750

Scene: Jerusalem

#1—Dramatic

Osman: Sultan of Jerusalem, in love with a Christian slave girl, 30s

Here, the powerful Sultan greets Zara and speaks of his love for her.

OSMAN: The sultans, my great ancestors, bequeath'd
Their empire to me, but their taste they gave not;
Their laws, their lives, their loves delight not me:
I know, our prophet smiles on am'rous wishes,
And opens a wide field to vast desire;
I know, that at my will I might possess;
That, wasting tenderness in wild profusion,
I might look down to my surrounded feet,
And bless contending beauties. I might speak,
Serenely slothful, from within my palace,
And bid my pleasure be my people's law.
But sweet as softness is, its end is cruel;
I can look 'round, and count a hundred kings,
Unconquer'd by themselves, and slaves to others:
Hence was Jerusalem to Christians lost;
"But Heaven, to blast that unbelieving race,
Taught me to be a king, by thinking like one."
Hence from the distant Euxine to the Nile,
The trumpet's voice has wak'd the world to war;
Yet, amidst arms and death, thy power has reach'd me;
For thou disdain'st, like me, a languid love;
Glory and Zara join—and charm together.

#2—Dramatic
    Osman

Osman has unjustly suspected Zara of falling in love with a European emissary to his court. When she protests her innocence, Osman regrets having doubted her love for him.

OSMAN: (Alone.) It should be yet, methinks, too soon to fly me!
Too soon as yet to wrong my easy faith.
The more I think, the less I can conceive,
What hidden cause should raise such strange despair!
Now, when her hopes have wings, and every wisk
Is courted to be lively!—When I love,
And joy and empire press her to their bosom;
"When not alone belov'd, but ev'n a lover:
Professing and accepting; bless'd and blessing;
To see her eyes, through tears, shine mystic love!
'Tis madness! and I were unworthy power,
To suffer longer the capricious insult!"
Yet, was I blameless?—No—I was too rash;
I have felt jealousy, and spoke it to her;
I have distrusted her—and still she loves:
Gen'rous atonement that! "and 'tis my duty
To expiate, by a length of soft indulgence,
The transports of a rage, which still was love.
Henceforth, I never will suspect her false;
Nature's plain power of charming dwells about her,
And innocence gives force to ev'ry word.
I owe full confidence to all she looks,
For in her eye shines truth, and ev'ry beam
Shoots confirmation 'round her."—I remark'd
Ev'n while she wept, her soul a thousand times
Sprung to her lips, and long'd to leap to mine,
With honest, ardent utt'rance of her love.—
Who can possess a heart so low, so base,
To look such tenderness, and yet have none?

The Virtuoso

Thomas Shadwell
1676

Scene: London

Serio-Comic
> Sir Formal Trifle: an orator and florid coxcomb, 40–50

> When Sir Formal is challenged to display his self-proclaimed talent for oration, he asks that a young lady in the company select the topic upon which he is to speak. Her choice? A mousetrap.

SIR FORMAL: I kiss your hand, madam. Now I am inspir'd with eloquence. Hem. Hem. Being one day, most noble auditors, musing in my study upon the too fleeting condition of poor humankind, I observed, not far from the scene of my meditation, an excellent machine call'd a mousetrap (which my man had plac'd there) which had included in it a solitary mouse, which pensive prisoner, in vain bewailing its own misfortunes and the precipitation of its too unadvised attempt, still struggling for liberty against the too stubborn opposition of solid wood and more obdurate wire; at last, the pretty malefactor having tir'd alas, its too feeble limbs till they became languid in fruitless endeavors for its excarceration, the pretty felon—since it could not break prison, and, its offence being beyond the benefit of the clergy, could hope for no bail—at last sat still, pensively lamenting the severity of its fate and narrowness of its, alas, too withering durance. After I had contemplated awhile upon the no little curiosity of the engine and the subtlety of its inventor, I began to reflect upon the enticement which so fatally betray'd the uncautious animal to its sudden ruin; and found it to be the too, alas, specious bait of Cheshire cheese, which seems to be a great delicate to the palate of this animal, who, in seeking to preserve its life, O misfortune, took the certain means to death, and searching for its livelihood had sadly encountered its own destruction.

The Wife of Bath

John Gay
1713

Scene: an inn lying on the road between London and Canterbury

#1—Serio-Comic
    Chaucer: a roguish con-man, 30–40

> Here, the rascally Chaucer makes overtures to Myrtilla, a fellow traveler while pretending to be a ghost.

CHAUCER: *Since the kind Stars to mutual love constrain,*
Why should the Tongue conceal our secret Pain?
Was it for this, inexorable Fair,
Your Magick drew me through the distant Air?
Tho' some curst Charm your wonted Speech denies,
At least shed Pity from those radiant Eyes,
And look me into Hope.—

In short, Madam, you see Destiny will have it so; and we have nothing else to do but submit.—Come, come, Madam, let us delay no Time, the Yoke of Matrimony sets best upon Young Shoulders.—Since the Tongue is upon the reserve, let us make use of the Lovers Language, and interpret by the Eyes;

> *We from the Ladies Eyes our Fate may learn,*
> *And in those Glasses Love or Hate discern.*

What, both your Tongue and Eyes under Command?—let me die if I do not think you the only Lady in Christendom that hath either of them in her Power.—I vow, Madam, you have an exquisite pretty Hand—so finely turn'd—

Chaucer here masquerades as a conjurer known as "Dr. Astrolabe" in order to further his suit with the unwitting Myrtilla.

CHAUCER: Yes, Madam, my Name is—Doc-tor *As-tro-labe*.—*Ger-ma-ny* has the Honour of my Birth, and *Scorpio* was Ascendant at my Nativity.—I am, Madam,—not only the seventh Son, but the Son of the seventh Son.—The occult Sciences have been my Study from the Cradle;—I have, my Lady,—by the Way, you see I can give you a Sketch of my Proficiency,—and show you that I am not unacquainted with your Quality.

[*BUSIE:* As I live, the Doctor is in the right of it.

MYRTILLA: Pray, cease your Impertinence, and be silent]

CHAUCER: I have, as I was saying, made practicable, and by great Labour and Application, brought to Perfection the Green and Hermetical Dragon;—'Twas owing to my indefatigable Searches, that the Female Fern-Seed was brought to light.—And if I can rely on some of the most plain *Phænomena*'s of Art, the Philosophers Stone will not lye long undiscover'd.—My Head, Madam, is a meer *Microcosm*,—or, if you please, like to Concave of the Heavens, lined with Planets, and powder'd with the Constellations.—Perhaps, before I fall directly on the Matter in hand, it will not be unnecessary to acquaint you with some of the Sciences that lye within the Circle of my Profession. *Astrology, Astronomy, Physick, Metaphysicks, Palmistry, Chiromancy, Physiognomy, Botany, Opticks, Catopticks, Diopticks, Necromancy, Divination, and Algebra.*—with several others, which at this time would be too tedious to recount.—Your Business, Madam, is inscrib'd in your Fore-head; and the Fates decree you Happiness.—though I must acquaint you, you seem to embrace it with Reluctance.